AUTHENTIC
ECOLODGES

AUTHENTIC ECOLODGES

Text and photography by Hitesh Mehta

Foreword by Costas Christ

Illustrations by Matthew Lewis

COLLINS DESIGN

An Imprint of HarperCollins *Publishers*

AUTHENTIC ECOLODGES

HarperCollins books may be purchased for educational,
business, or sales promotional use. For information, please write:
Special Markets Department, HarperCollins*Publishers*,
10 East 53rd Street, New York, NY 10022.

First published in 2010 by:
Collins Design,
An Imprint of HarperCollins*Publishers*
10 East 53rd Street
New York, NY 10022
Tel: (212) 207–7000
Fax: (212) 207–7654
collinsdesign@harpercollins.com
www.harpercollins.com

Distributed throughout the world by:
HarperCollins*Publishers*
10 East 53rd Street
New York, NY 10022
Fax: (212) 207–7654
Library of Congress Control Number: 2010925739
ISBN 978-0-06-168843-0

Designed by Agnieszka Stachowicz

Printed in China
First Printing, 2010

DEDICATED TO ZORBA, WHO TAUGHT ME HOW TO UNCONDITIONALLY LOVE ALL SPECIES, AND BIMAL, WHO, IN THE EARLY 1980S, HELPED ME IN MY INITIAL LODGE-LEARNING YEARS.

CONTENTS

FOREWORD

The first time it entered my mind that tourism needed a serious make-over, I was standing on the roof of a Land Rover watching Samburu National Reserve—an arid slice of savannah in Kenya's northern frontier where rare wildlife and camera-wielding tourists roam—go up in flames. It was 1979 and I had embarked on a career as a wildlife biologist as part of a Harvard University project to study vervet monkeys. Instead, I found a brewing conflict between the local Samburu tribe and the reserve named after them, carved out of land they once owned. This was the heyday of mass wildlife tourism in East Africa and safari companies were raking in millions of dollars, but the Samburu saw none of the benefit. Frustrated by this injustice, they'd rather imprudently set the reserve on fire. I watched wind-stoked flames devour the vegetation, sending gerenuks, impalas, and giraffes fleeing to safer ground. The park rangers, some in bare feet, radioed for help in fighting the blaze. The irony hit me. This multi-million dollar industry left the rangers helpless, disturbed the wildlife, and disenfranchised the local people.

As I lived out my days along the Uaso Nyiro River, I envisioned a different kind of tourism—a tourism that could directly support the well-being of the local people and make a real contribution to protecting nature. I spent the following years pursuing this vision in Africa and elsewhere, along with others who sought a new tourism horizon. Out efforts would lead to the birth of the ecotourism movement.

To be sure, ecotourism has had a difficult journey. While nature travel boomed in the 1980s, the tenets of ecotourism were slow to take root. In 1990, when a dozen scientists, conservationists, and tour operators from around the world gathered in a farm house outside of Washington, D.C., for the inaugural meeting of The International Ecotourism Society, our first task was to define what, exactly, ecotourism was. We decided on the following definition: Responsible travel to natural areas that conserves the environment and improves the well-being of local people. None of us, however, knew of a real working model of it anywhere.

It was around this same time—an experimental period when ecotourism was long on promises but short on delivery—that I met a Kenyan-born architect and landscape architect named Hitesh Mehta. I was impressed by his genuine desire to make ecotourism really work. He understood what was at stake: a rapidly growing tourism industry that was expanding each year into the world's last strongholds of wilderness, home to rare and endangered species and the make-or-break world of basic survival for millions of people in Africa, Asia, and the Americas. If we did not get tourism development right, it ran the risk of destroying the very cultural and natural attractions that visitors came to see. I am happy to report that trial and error has led to mounting success, with Hitesh Mehta playing a vital role in that process.

Authentic Ecolodges brings this success to the page in brilliant images and informative descriptions of thirty-six ecolodges that stand out as among the very best in the world. They represent geographic diversity, innovative designs, and different habitats, ranging from desert to rainforest. I like to think of this book as the tasting menu to a great Michelin star restaurant—sustainable cuisine, of course—where every dish is carefully prepared using the finest local ingredients, expertly combined to compliment each other, and individually cooked to order so that no two items are alike. If you get to personally experience even just one of the lodges found on the following pages, running the full spectrum from budget to luxury, you will experience true ecotourism, where the guest, the natural environment, and the local people come together to deliver a positive return on life —a rewarding travel experience that also gives back to the planet.

It is fair to say that what started as ecotourism two decades ago has given rise to what may be the most significant transformation in the history of modern travel—the emergence of sustainable tourism. While ecotourism focuses on nature in the far-flung corners of the globe, sustainable tourism is taking the same principles and practices of being environmentally friendly, supporting the economic and social well-being of local communities, and helping to protect cultural and natural heritage, and moving them into the tourism mainstream. We are now at a global tipping point where new innovations are happening almost daily—major airports touting shielded light fixtures to reduce nighttime light pollution, urban hotels switching to in-room utensils made from biodegradable potato starch instead of plastic, and the emergence of organic golf resorts where harmful pesticides and herbicides are a thing of the past, to cite a few examples. While there is still a lot more that needs to be done, one thing is certain: The question is no longer can sustainable tourism work. It does. Rather, the question now is how far we can take it to transform the global travel industry into a catalyst for helping to protect nature and safeguard culture diversity for future generations. *Authentic Ecolodges* is helping to take us there.

—Costas Christ

INTRODUCTION

WELCOME TO THE VIBRANT, EXOTIC, AND ALTRUISTIC WORLD OF *AUTHENTIC ECOLODGES*.

In 2007, I left my full-time job as a landscape architect, environmental planner, and architect with a Florida-based firm to focus all of my attention producing the book you now have in your hands. And while this project has indeed been among the most ambitious of my life, I can't say that it wasn't without its perks—minus the constant jet lag, of course. In the course of three years, I embarked on a life-changing journey that took me to forty-six countries, spanning six continents, to research the ecolodges presented here. In total, I visited forty-four lodges, and in some instances, I made repeat visits, if only to confirm what I already knew: The thirty-six ecolodges collected in this book are among the most authentic in the world; their visitor experiences are simply unrivaled. Why did I visit each lodge? For a book that prides itself on being authentic, the ecolodges presented here are only as good as my word. It is one thing to read press releases about ecotourism and ecolodges, and quite another to visit the locales and experience them firsthand. Admittedly, there were moments of inspired relaxation, so trust me, dear reader: My research has benefited me as much as it does you. So what, you may be wondering aloud, is the definition of an ecolodge, and what makes it "authentic"?

After ten years of research, interviews with architects, eco-consultants, developers, operators, many indigenous communities, and feedback from stakeholders in the ecotourism industry, I developed the following definition: An ecolodge is a two- to seventy-five room, low-impact, nature-based, financially sustainable accommodation facility that helps protect sensitive neighboring areas; involves and helps benefit local communities; offers tourists an interpretive and interactive participatory experience; provides a spiritual communion with nature and culture; and is planned, designed, constructed, and operated in an environmentally and socially sensitive manner. I then developed the following criteria to determine authenticity. First and foremost, an authentic ecolodge *must* embody the three main principles of ecotourism: 1) nature must be protected and conserved 2) through community outreach and education programs, local community must benefit 3) interpretive programs must be offered to educate both tourists and employees about the surrounding natural and cultural environments.

Following these principles, then, an ecolodge must satisfy two additional criteria from this list of eight:

1. Use alternative and sustainable means of water acquisition and at the same time reduce overall water consumption.

2. Meet its energy needs through passive design and renewable sources.

3. Provide for careful handling (reduce, refuse, recycle, reuse) and disposal of solid waste.

4. Use environmentally friendly sewage treatment systems.

5. Fit into its specific physical and cultural contexts through careful attention to form, landscaping, and color as well as through the use of vernacular architecture.

6. Use environmentally friendly building and furnishings materials.

7. Have minimal impact on the natural surroundings and utilize traditional building techniques during construction.

8. Endeavor to work with the local community, including community members, wherever possible, in the initial physical planning and design stages of construction.

Every lodge I visited was subjected to the above criteria system. My verification process included on-site investigations and exhaustive interviews with local community members, lodge owners/operators, and local government officials. This is the first time in the history of tourism that one person has visited every single property and objectively used one criteria system to verify the authenticity of the accommodation facility. It is impossible for one ecolodge to satisfy every tenet of this system, and failure to do so is not based on intent, but more often than not on physical and cultural limitation. If an accommodation facility is located near a fresh water river or in a rain forest, for example, it's not necessary to spend money on water conservation technologies. Similarly, in some areas, local building material may not be available. Therefore, it may be prudent to import environmentally friendly foreign materials.

The thirty-six ecolodges presented in this book have satisfied the five points of the criteria system and are, therefore, considered authentic. Their evolution in the field of ecotourism has never been charted—until now. Each entry is awarded a score, indicated by butterfly symbols, in a rating system that directly correlates to a lodge's individual metamorphosis toward total sustainability. Think of these butterflies as indicators of ecological and social enlightenment, with each butterfly representing a stage of a seven-tiered development phase, the first stage having satisfied all five criteria indentified above. It is my sincerest hope that proprietors, architects, academics, and travelers will reference this system and use it to track the continued evolution of ecolodges around the world in their quest for environmental, social, and spiritual refinement.

Authentic Ecolodges is broken into twelve theme-based chapters. Within each chapter, there are three highlighted ecolodges that best represent a chapter's given theme. Comprehensive text places the photographs, illustrations, and site plans into proper context and gives an overview of the ecolodge's personality as well as its main features and information about guest activities and cuisine.

For the traveler in you, do know that your accommodation choice can make a huge difference, both to the local communities and to the conservation of fragile ecosystems. Through this book, it is my wish that I can be, as Gandhi said, "the change that I would like to see in the world." It is my sincerest hope that you enjoy *Authentic Ecolodges*, whether you read it cover to cover or casually peruse its pages from time to time. Please visit the book's Web site, www.authenticecolodges, to send me your comments.

For the earth,
Hitesh Mehta

A note regarding the photography: Several different cameras (traditional SLR and digital) were used for this book. I started with a traditional SLR (Nikon N80) and slide transparencies, then switched to a semi-professional digital (Nikon D200), and finally upgraded to the professional Nikon D700. A few of the photos in this book are also taken with a Canon Powershot Sub-Compact. Several different lenses were utilized: For long distance shots, a 200-400mm f/5.6 Tamron zoom lens; for middle-distance and portraits, a 70-300mm Nikkor f/4 zoom lens; for wide angle shots, a 12-24mm Nikkor f/4 zoom lens, and for close-ups, Micro-Nikkor 60mm and 105mm f/2.8 lenses. For extreme close-ups, I used the Nikon Ring-Flash system and for fill-in flash, I used SB-800 and SB-900 flashes. Most photos were taken with tripods and in many cases using remote-shutters. Finally, to re-create what one would see with the naked eye, some photos were touched-up using Lightroom, Photoshop, and Helicon Filter software.

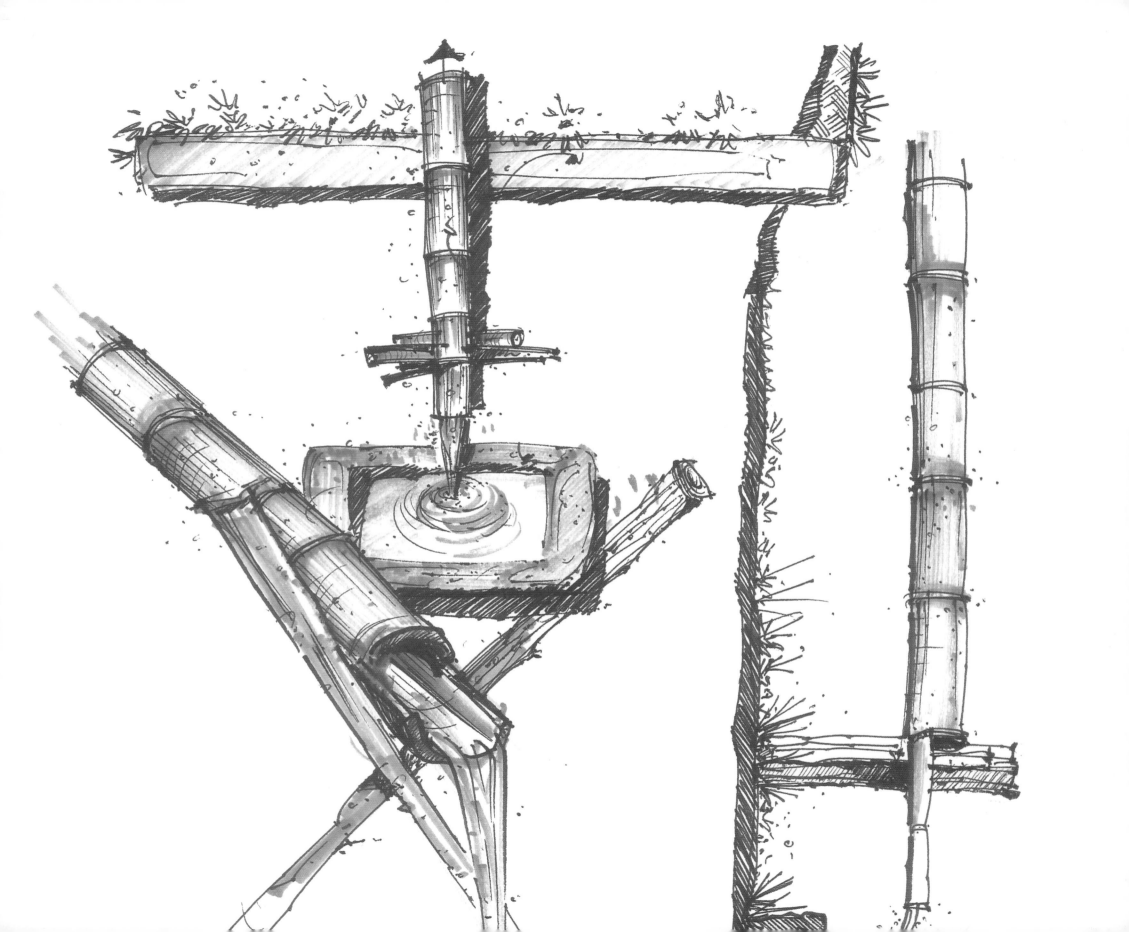

SUSTAINABLE BUILDING MATERIALS

The sustainability of an ecolodge can be determined, in part, by its choice of building materials. Exemplary scenarios for ecolodges involve combinations of traditional and modern building materials that have the least ecological impact and are both efficient and maintenance friendly. In the most optimal scenario, traditional building materials should be sourced locally; their use should benefit the local economy, generate local hand labor, reduce transportation costs and pollution as well as the need for heavy and noisy building plants and equipment. In instances where traditional building materials aren't available, innovative environmentally friendly materials—ceramic tiles made from crushed light bulbs and recycled clay, for example—can substitute. The most authentic ecolodges, like the three highlighted in this chapter, set the standard in terms of using building materials that are abundant and renewable, and whose manufacture has a low impact on the environment from where it has originated.

Each material has its own message. Bring out the nature of the materials, let their nature intimately into your scheme. Form and function thus become one in design and execution if the nature of materials and method and purpose are all in unison.
—Frank Lloyd Wright

CROSSWATERS ECOLODGE

NANKUNSHAN RESERVE, GUANGDONG, CHINA

DATE COMPLETED
2007

OWNER
Patten Xu (China)

MASTER PLANNER AND
LANDSCAPE ARCHITECT
EDSA (United States)

ARCHITECTS
Paul Pholeros (Australia)
Simón Vélez (Colombia)
Hitesh Mehta (Kenya/United States)
Ken Luoguiqin (China)

INTERIOR DESIGNER
Buz Design Consultants Ltd. (Hong Kong)

LIGHTING DESIGNER
Linbeck Rausch Ltd. (Hong Kong)

FÊNG SHUI CONSULTANT
Michael Chiang (Hong Kong)

ECOLOGIST
Professor Zhen Li (China)

BOTANIST
Professor Xing Fuwu (China)

HORTICULTURALIST
Feng Ding (China)

ORNITHOLOGIST
Professor Gao Yu-Ren (China)

Previous spread: The ecolodge in situ, Nankunshan Reserve, a 3,000 acre national reserve created in 1993. Opposite, left: A view of the Lotus Garden and covered walkway from the Bamboo Pavilion. Right: Lush, natural bamboo forest surroundings inspire meditative thought. This page: Covered bamboo walkway and electric cart path that service the river villas hidden behind the vegetation.

The synthesis of sustainability and elegant design, Crosswaters Ecolodge is poised at the crossroads of civilization (Hong Kong, Shenzhen, and Guangzhou) and nature (the Nankunshan Nature Reserve in Central Guangdong Province in South China). Home to over two thousand types of plants and animals, Nankunshan is a veritable natural wonderland. It is often referred to as "an oasis on the Tropic of Cancer" and "nature's oxygen bar," in tribute to its pure, clean air, despite its proximity to one of the world's most crowded—and hazy—regions. Undisturbed by the pollution and noise of southern China, Crosswaters' holistic approach to sustainable living is all the more remarkable.

As the first master-planned ecolodge in China, it's fitting that the three-year-old Crosswaters is built on fundamental fêng shui principles and principally features bamboo—the country's ultimate renewable building material. Virtually everything in Crosswaters—from its stunning bridge and covered walkways, to lodge building roofs and the floors

themselves—is constructed from the material, making Crosswaters the world's largest example of the use of bamboo in a commercial project. The use of locally accessed material isn't isolated to bamboo, however. Local earth, clay, marble, river stone, and flora are also used, and several of the building materials are refurbished, recycled, and reused: The boardwalks, for example, are made of abandoned railroad ties, while roof tiles are from previously demolished buildings in the nearby Shangping village.

Designed to be harmoniously integrated with the local culture as well as the natural surroundings, Crosswaters ingeniously employs the principles of fêng shui in its planning and design blueprint. Advised by a fêng shui master—who massaged a conceptual site plan specifically designed to help harness the chi (spiritual energy) of the location—the landscape architectural team situated the lodge's buildings in the most desirable fêng shui configuration: the hills to their back, the water to their front. If this weren't indication enough

Above: Moon Reflection Pool and Lounge/Bar. Opposite, clockwise from top left: Bamboo and granite-inspired Poet's Fountain. Poetry depicts traditional romanticism toward landscape; A wall constructed with reused clay roof tiles, rammed earth, and river stones; Guests at the ecolodge visit with local villagers; Vibrantly colored lotus flowers blossom in the summer. Following page, top: View of Bamboo Bridge from the main restaurant. Bottom, left: Bedroom, Single River Villa. Center: Bird's-eye view of the Gankeng River from the Observation Tower. Right: Guest Welcome Center. Electric cart boardwalk is constructed from abandoned railroad ties.

that everything—from the spiritual to the material—has been attended to at Crosswaters, the lodge's subtle design details speak volumes, the likes of which include low-wattage lights that gently illuminate the covered walkways that are reminiscent of those found at Beijing's Summer Palace and Suzhou's ancient gardens. The riverfront villas themselves are built in a style conforming to traditional Hakka structures with raised roofs and mud walls, and are luxuriously appointed with local textiles.

Cocooned within a natural kingdom of montane forest and situated at the junction of the Gankengmei and Sumaoping rivers, Crosswaters is a well-balanced ecolodge that answers both the luxury needs of a high-end boutique lodge and the sustainability beliefs of ecotourism. It is, quite simply, the epitome of Tao—transcendence of all duality, transcendence of all polarity, transcendence of all opposites. Where yin and yang are in dynamic equilibrium.

CUISINE: All vegetables and herbs used in the Crosswaters kitchen are sourced locally. The kitchen specializes in Hakka fare, using ingredients such as fresh young bamboo shoots and tofu, for which this area of China is known. Western-style fine dining is also available.

ACTIVITIES: Besides bird-watching excursions in the surrounding protected forests and plenty of stargazing opportunities via a high-definition telescope, guests can learn to cook Nankun cakes, the local delicacy. The Crosswaters Forest Spa's comprehensive therapeutic approach includes an array of specialty treatments, like the green tea and chrysanthemum scrub. The treatment ingredients are natural products found within Nankunshan: bamboo, honey, nectar, and alkaline-free cocoa tea.

何处深春好
春深种莳家
唐刘禹锡
分畦接树
般字水
花分畦

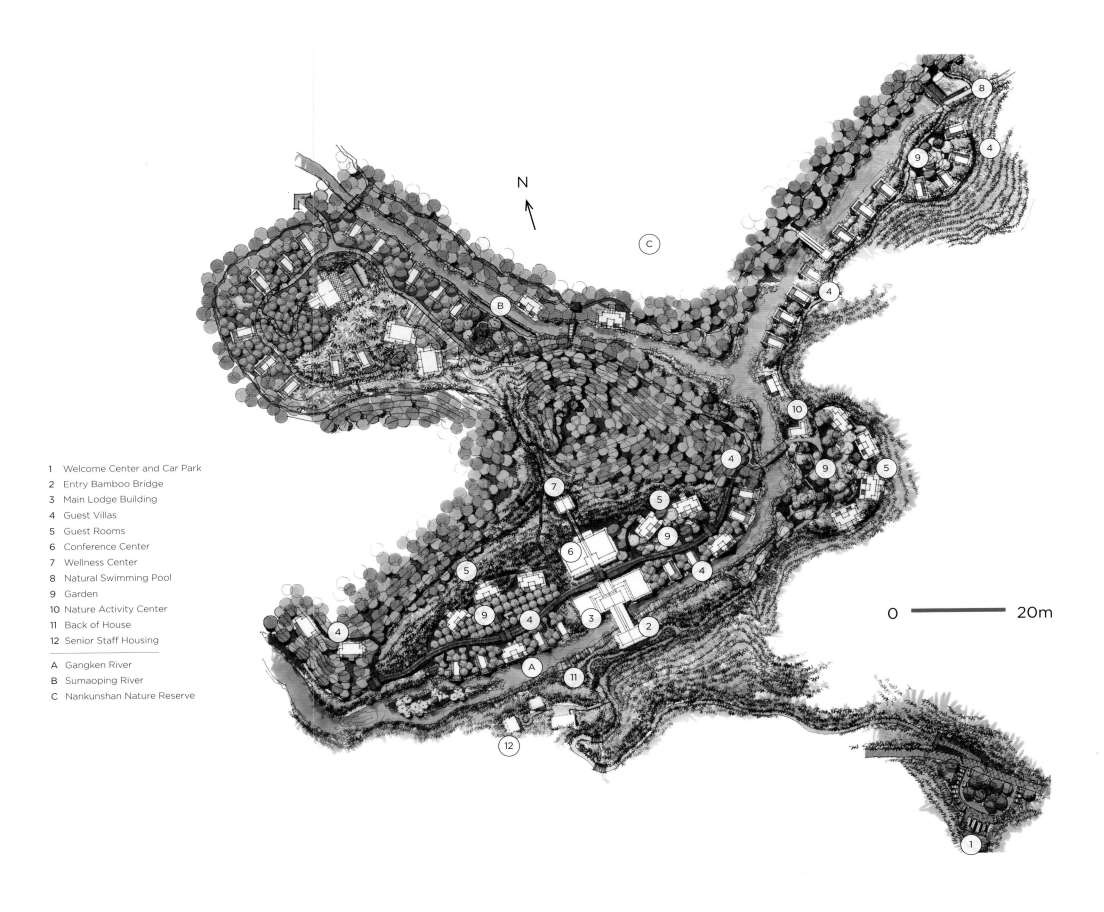

1 Welcome Center and Car Park
2 Entry Bamboo Bridge
3 Main Lodge Building
4 Guest Villas
5 Guest Rooms
6 Conference Center
7 Wellness Center
8 Natural Swimming Pool
9 Garden
10 Nature Activity Center
11 Back of House
12 Senior Staff Housing

A Gangken River
B Sumaoping River
C Nankunshan Nature Reserve

N

0 ——— 20m

URUYÉN LODGE

CANAIMA NATIONAL PARK, VENEZUELA

DATE COMPLETED
1995

OWNER
Carballo Martinez Family

DESIGNER
Henrique Carballo

The name Uruyén was derived from the mythical story of Yurwan (meaning "big fish" in local Pemón language). It is also the famous site where the legendary explorers Jimmie Angel and Ruth Robertson set up base camps back in the 1930s and 1940s respectively before their expeditions to Angel Falls—the highest falls in the world. Accessible only by a small plane or helicopter, Uruyén Lodge is situated in a savannah ecosystem deep in Canaima National Park. Here, twelve Native American *churuatas* (typical indigenous dwellings) are nestled alongside the Yurwan River, set against the majestic foothill of the flat-topped Auyan Tepuy (Devil's Mountain).

The round, palm-thatched dwellings of Uruyén Lodge are models of indigenous construction, and made entirely of sustainable materials. The roof is made of palm fronds from the Moriche Palm, known by locals as the "tree of life." The wood—all the columns and the roof rafters—is sourced from cartan, a plant from the rain forest, and mud is sourced on-site.

Inside, the furnishings are simple; the beds, tables, and wardrobes are all made out of locally sourced wood while the hammocks are made from local woven cloth. As the traditional architecture of the local Pémon Native Americans, the comfortable churuatas set the tone for an authentic ecolodge experience.

Owned and operated by the Pémon family of Carballo Martinez, Uruyén Lodge is completely solar powered and has no generator. The refrigerator and stoves are gas powered, and all lighting is compact fluorescent. The innovative outdoor shower uses minimal water, which is sourced directly from the nearby river. Additionally, no trees were cut and no machinery was used during the construction of the lodge. With few luxuries, this lodge is best suited for those who crave adventure amid the outdoors.

Uruyén Lodge is located in beautiful Kamarata Valley and within walking distance of local Pemón villages of Old Uruyén, Santa Marta, Kavak, and Kamarata. The area is idyllically situated,

Previous spread: The lodge in situ, alongside the Yurwan River, in Canaima National Park. Opposite: Visitors set out for the internationally recognized day hike to Kavak village and lodge. This page, left: View from the ecolodge of Auyan Tepuy (Devil's Mountain). Right: Angel Falls, the highest uninterrupted waterfalls on the planet.

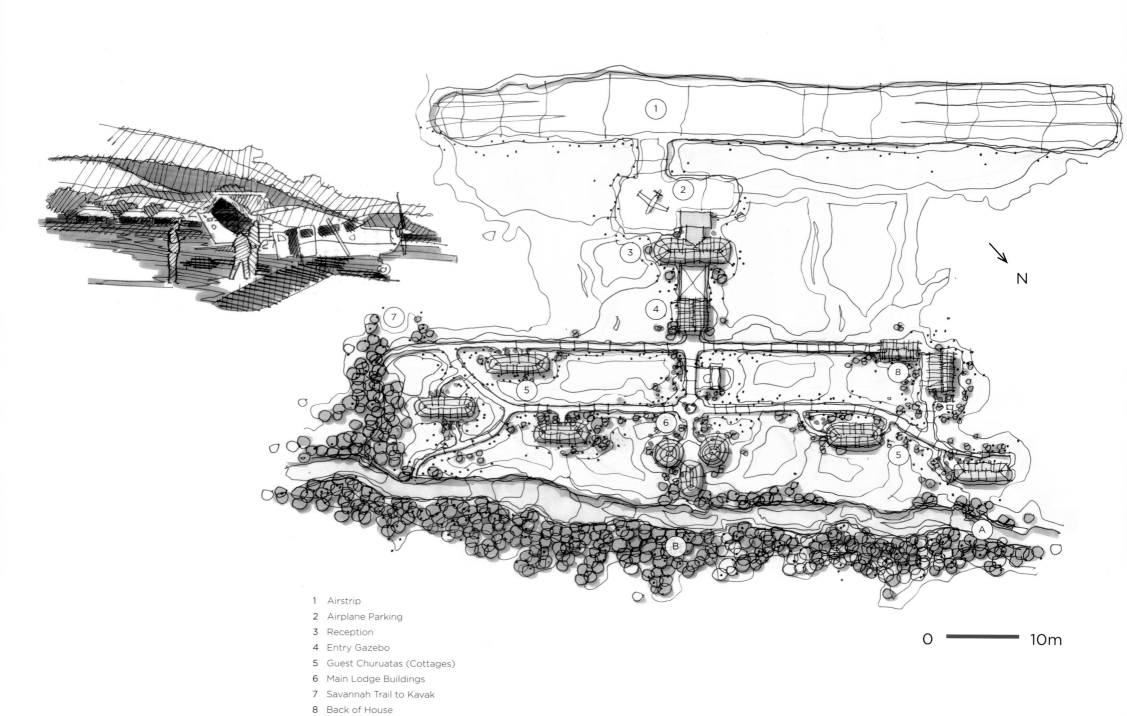

1 Airstrip

2 Airplane Parking

3 Reception

4 Entry Gazebo

5 Guest Churuatas (Cottages)

6 Main Lodge Buildings

7 Savannah Trail to Kavak

8 Back of House

A Yurwan River

B Canaima National Park

N

0 ——— 10m

with a range of hiking trails in just about every direction: Half-day trips can be organized to the Uruyén Canyon, one-day trips to the Kavak Waterfalls and Caves, and four-hour trips to the Guayaraca lookout point, a plateau 500 meters (one-third mile) around the lodge that offers stunning views of the Gran Sabana (savannah). With only thirty beds (ten in hammocks) available, the Uruyén is a remote getaway. Hidden among the foothills of the Auyan Tepuy, it is a rustic gem that offers absolute immersion in nature and the local culture.

ACTIVITIES: Trek to the top of Auyan Tepuy (six days) following the route Jimmy Angel used after his plane crashed on the summit while he was searching for the "river of gold," go by boat to visit Angel Falls (five days), or hike to the Aicha Tepuy (three days) and continue to the Pur Pur Valley (three days). Boat rides to Canaima through the Akanan and Carrao rivers are also available. Other activities include bird-watching, swimming, and kayaking in the Aicha River.

Clockwise from left: Local canoe ride along the Aicha River; Indigenous Pemón children performing a dance around a fire; The underside of the Moriche palm-thatched and cartan-rafter roof of the main lodge building at Uruyén.

FEYNAN ECOLODGE

DANA NATURE RESERVE, JORDAN

DATE COMPLETED
2005

OWNER
Royal Society of the Conservation of Nature (RSCN)

ARCHITECT
Ammar Khammash Architects (Jordan)

As the most impoverished people in Jordan, the indigenous Bedouin communities have few options for sustainable living. Their survival is dependent upon the goat, whose population gets more and more scarce every year due to overgrazing. The Royal Society for the Conservation of Nature (RSCN) was created to protect the native ecosystems. In trying to reduce the effects of overgrazing, the society developed several ideas to provide alternative sources of income for the Bedouin. Enter Feynan Ecolodge, which is located within the Dana Nature Reserve, a pristine 200 square kilometer (116 square mile) area with diverse habitats and animal species. The ecolodge helps raise funds for the reserve and also provides employment opportunities for local Bedouins.

Located at the western end of the reserve, the lodge is usually reached via a two-and-a-half-hour drive from the capital, Amman, to the lodge reception in Rashaidi village. Then it takes another half hour in a local Bedouin truck over a rough road. Alternately, the lodge can be reached by a five-hour walk down through the gorge of Wadi Dana to the desert floor at Feynan. The journey to Feynan Ecolodge, however, is just the beginning of the adventures that await. Whether partaking in a hike led by a local ecoguide, riding a camel through the picturesque desert valley, visiting Bedouin homes for a sampling of local culture, or simply conversing with the 90 percent Bedouin staff, guests are submerged in the authentic Bedouin lifestyle.

With a color palette that mirrors the hue of the surrounding cliffs, Feynan Ecolodge blends organically and unobtrusively into its desert surroundings and looks as though it has risen from the land itself. Built entirely by locals and utilizing a unique arabesque-like design created by well-known local architect Ammar Khammash, the lodge incorporates traditional adobe-type building techniques and environmentally friendly materials: The walls, for example, are made of hollow block, straw bale, and have a mud finish.

Previous spread: The lodge in situ, surrounded by Bedouin tents deep in the mountainous Dana Biosphere Reserve. Opposite page, clockwise from top left: The candle-lit reception and lobby; Native Bedouin girl from a village close to the Feynan Ecolodge; Lodge guest enjoying a traditional vegetarian meal at the lodge restaurant; Rugged desert landscape; Deluxe candle-lit suite has a balcony overlooking the desert and wadi. This page: Balcony and exterior views of the lodge.

Above: Guests can get rejuvenated in the therapeutic Dead Sea on their way to Feynan Ecolodge.
Right: The porosity of the ecolodge is best exemplified through this bird's-eye view of the domed rooms and roof terraces.

The terraces are covered with stones from the desert floor and all the lodge furnishings and fittings were constructed using local materials.

The lodge's twenty-six rooms and all the public areas, such as the lounge and dining room, are candlelit by night, creating a romantic and ambient mood. The roof includes some eighty-plus solar panels that provide hot water for showers and electric power to the kitchen and to bathroom lights. Passively designed internal courtyards assist in creating cross ventilation and cooler temperatures while dual-flush toilets help conserve water, a precious resource in this desert environment.

CUISINE: Since meat and chicken require energy-guzzling freezers, Feynan Ecolodge serves only vegetarian food, which is incredibly authentic: freshly made apricot juice; superb local products like *hallawiye*, honey, and cheese; excellent dinner dishes, such as Bukhari, *shanklesh*, and *fatush* served with Bedouin bread. Breakfasts include locally made jam, yogurts (both salty and sweet), olive oil, *za'atar*, eggs, olives, and dates.

ACTIVITIES: Beyond the hiking and camel riding, guests can indulge themselves in a romantic Bedouin tent experience, complete with serenading oud and flute players. The local Bedouin staff give guided tours through the beautiful as well as fascinating surroundings, where guests can find Bronze Age remains of copper ovens and Roman and Byzantine ruins. A variety of unmarked trails provide local and long-distance treks, including ones to Dana Village and Petra.

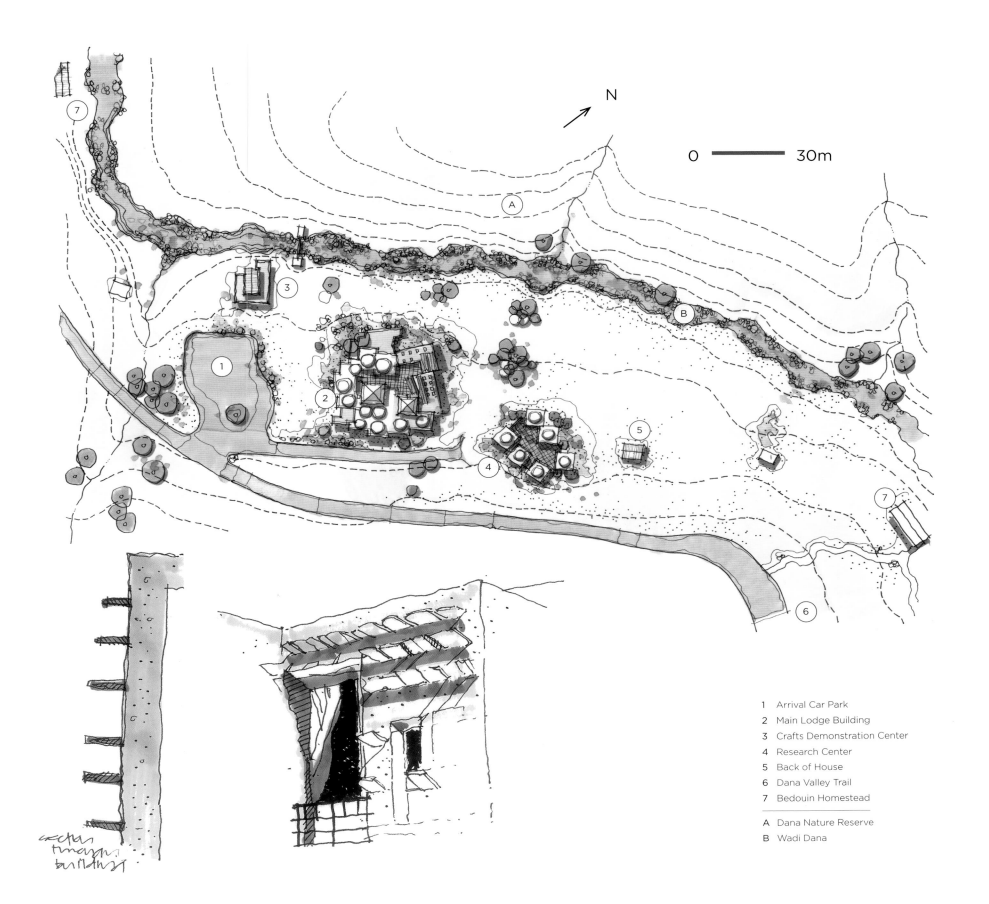

N

0 ——— 30m

1 Arrival Car Park
2 Main Lodge Building
3 Crafts Demonstration Center
4 Research Center
5 Back of House
6 Dana Valley Trail
7 Bedouin Homestead

A Dana Nature Reserve
B Wadi Dana

CREATIVE DESIGN

The three case studies presented here are exemplary models of creative design elements in that they all successfully accomplish three goals: 1) the architecture and design work in harmony with either the physical or cultural context of the area 2) the building materials and construction were light on the land and 3) the construction techniques were innovative. The architectural forms of each lodge seamlessly interact with the surrounding ecological and geological features, blending into them wherever possible. As visual extensions of the natural landscape, then, these three lodges are visually sustainable structures, timeless in their beauty, design ingenuity, and holistic approach to their environment, climate, and culture.

Making the simple complicated is commonplace; making the complicated simple, awesomely simple, that's creativity.
—Charles Mingus

SHOMPOLE

GREAT RIFT VALLEY, KENYA

DATE COMPLETED
2001

OWNERS
Art of Ventures and Local Loodokilani Maasai Clan

DESIGNERS
Anthony Russell (Kenya) and Neil Retcher (Kenya)

S ituated within a 12,140 hectare (30,000 acre) private wildlife conservancy on the edge of the Nguruman Escarpment in Southern Kenya, and just north of the flamingo-rich Lake Natron, Shompole delivers an authentic ecolodge safari experience. Vast, wooded, semiarid savannah plains are punctuated by the volcanic hills of the Great Rift Valley, providing Shompole with a never-ending palette of natural colors, textures, and materials with which to work. The nine-villa and one private house ecolodge is the product of a unique partnership between the local community, which owns a 30 percent share, and the private investor/operator Art of Ventures, which owns the remaining 70 percent. The conservancy and Maasai Group Ranch provide an important migratory corridor for elephants, and is one of few places in the world where guests can see four species of hyena. In an effort to preserve and protect the environment, Shompole works with the local Maasai communities to create tangible ways for them to benefit from sustainable use of natural resources.

Not only is Shompole's overall philosophy toward conservation inspirational, so too is their approach to sensitive architectural design. Drawing their creative design cues from the surrounding landscape, Shompole's visionary architecture exists in harmony with the southern Kenya landscape, and in this area, Shompole is a model of accomplishment. Constructed using naturally occurring white quartz stone, pale thatch grass, and fig wood, each villa provides a spacious oasis in the arid environment. There are no doors or windows in any of the private or public rooms and this not only creates "passive design" airflow, but it also helps provide guests with a refreshing spiritual communion with nature. From the contemporary guest villas—left completely open to the elements save a mosquito net and palm-thatched roofing—to the water paths that wind their way through individual villas and collect into private free form pools, every aspect about Shompole is meant to impress. Created with a rare sense of design integrity few ecolodges

Previous spread: The lodge in situ, overlooking the Great Rift Valley hills and with Lake Natron in the horizon. Opposite: Little Shompole villa overlooking the woodland savannah at sunrise. This page, left: Water is a main feature of the property, flowing through each room and collecting in private pools. Above: Local Loodokilani village boy, a shareholder in the ecolodge.

Above: Innovative architectural elements include white quartz stone, palm thatch, polished fig wood, and white-and-black cement flooring. Opposite: Living and sleeping area of the Private Suite of Little Shompole.

possess, Shompole epitomizes the height of luxurious living with a distinctly Kenyan flavor.

Divided into three sections—Shompole, Little Shompole, and Private House—the ecolodge is strategically sited to overlook the Lake Natron basin, ensuring ample opportunities for sunrise and moonrise watching, all from the privacy of one's individual guest villa. Little Shompole consists of two ample-sized private villa suites within walking distance of the main Shompole Lodge. Accommodation at Little Shompole is equipped with an exclusive entourage of staff, including a private guide and butler. The recently (2008) built two-bedroom Shompole Private House takes the innovative design that has become synonymous with Shompole to new heights. Equipped with energy-saving lights and solar-powered showers and water pumps, the Private House strives to reduce energy consumption while providing comfort to guests.

Built with inspiration, innovation, and integrity, and featuring structures that seem to vanish into the landscape,

Shompole elevates ecoconsciousness into a novel state of luxury that is accomplished with smart, creative design.

CUISINE: Shompole runs a full-fledged in-house organic garden, which provides 15 percent of the lodge's fruit and vegetable needs. The rest comes from local farmers and Nairobi. Freshly prepared healthy fusion dishes are the order of the day, but for special occasions, the lodge organizes candlelit bush dinners under the stars.

ACTIVITIES: There is no shortage of activities for the adventurous guest. River canoeing, mountain hiking, and wildlife watching (either at night or by day) are just a sampling of the many things to do while experiencing the Shompole-inspired Kenyan safari experience. For those in need of solitude and private contemplation, the plains and endless sky stir the meditative spirit like nothing else.

Above: The lodge's location in a private conservancy affords ample opportunity to take in the sights of indigenous wildlife, either from specially modified safari 4 x 4 vehicles or from the comfort of your room. Right: The perfect place for watching the sunset.

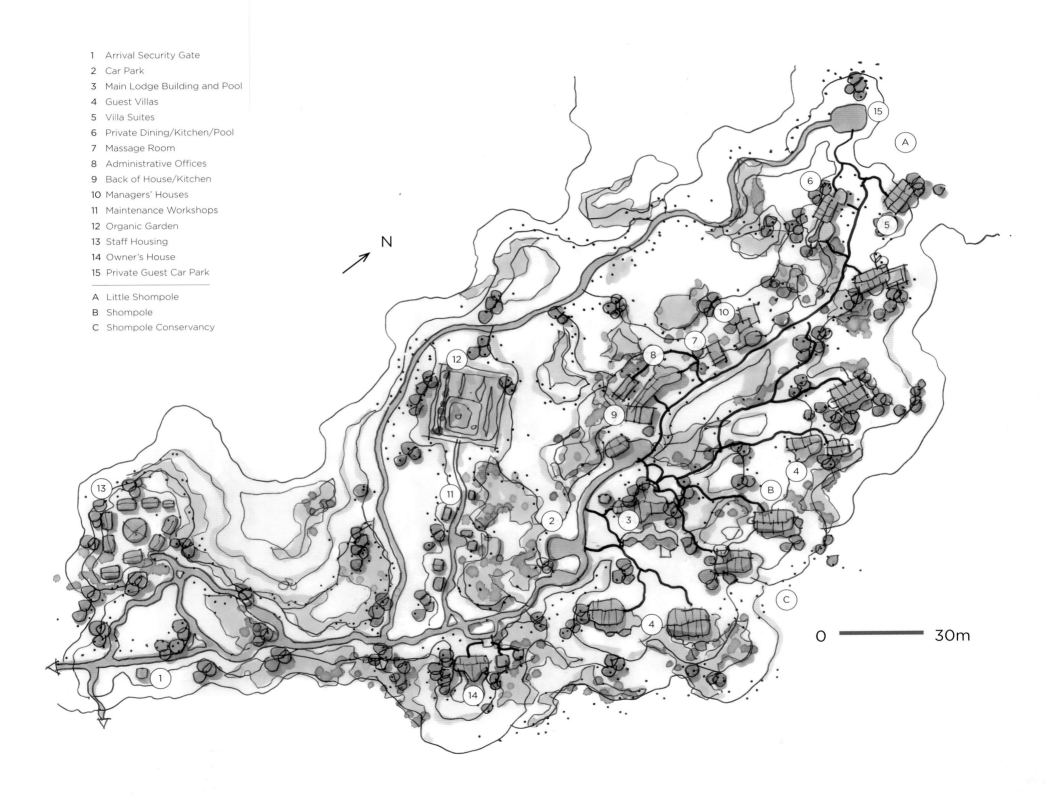

1 Arrival Security Gate
2 Car Park
3 Main Lodge Building and Pool
4 Guest Villas
5 Villa Suites
6 Private Dining/Kitchen/Pool
7 Massage Room
8 Administrative Offices
9 Back of House/Kitchen
10 Managers' Houses
11 Maintenance Workshops
12 Organic Garden
13 Staff Housing
14 Owner's House
15 Private Guest Car Park

A Little Shompole
B Shompole
C Shompole Conservancy

N

0 ▬▬▬▬ 30m

BAY OF FIRES LODGE

TASMANIA, AUSTRALIA

DATE COMPLETED
2000

OWNER
Anthology Pty. Ltd.

ARCHITECT
Ken Latona (Australia)

The "walkabout" is a genuinely Aboriginal concept: a short period of wandering bush life as an occasional interruption of regular work. It is apt, then, that Bay of Fires Lodge is reachable only by a two-day hike through the Mount William National Park. As far as walkabouts go, this is by far among the world's most experiential, not only for its scenery and interpretation, but also for what awaits at journey's end: an architecturally stunning lodge every bit as dramatic as the surrounding landscape.

Designed by Ken Latona, Bay of Fires Lodge lives up to the architect's motto to "touch the earth lightly." Completely self-sustaining, the lodge features composting toilets and solar power–generated appliances, and captures rainwater for reuse. Harmoniously nestled between ocean and bush and speckled with casuarina trees, the lodge is a striking marriage of inspired architecture and ecoconsciousness. Latona explains, "You can get the environmental criteria right, but you can miss the emotional response to a place. If you

walk into a place and it affects you in some way, then it's probably a pretty successful piece of architecture. When it lifts the spirit, you know." With its pitched roof—designed to deflect inclement weather across the building—and its all-glass enclosures, the lodge is light and airy inside. Exposed laminated beams and glass louvers reflect the horizon line of the ocean, and long timber outdoor decks welcome uninterrupted views of the hardscrabble vista. Bay of Fires Lodge is creative design at its best.

For its loftlike architecture, Bay of Fires Lodge stays grounded with its strong connection to the land and its people. During the planning stages, for example, approval was sought from the Aboriginal Land Council before siting the building; much of the land is home to local sacred Aboriginal sites. And during construction, building materials were mainly flown in by helicopter—only four trees were removed—further proof that Bay of Fires Lodge is infused with a light touch, indeed. The lodge buildings

Previous spread: The lodge in situ, deep in the woods surrounding Mount William National Park. Opposite, top: Environmentally friendly hardwood and plantation pine were used to construct the pathways and stairs. Bottom, left: White sandy beaches, granite outcrops, and a dramatic coastline make for the ultimate Robinson Crusoe–like day adventure. Center: Floor-to-ceilings windows in the ocean-facing library welcome in tons of natural light. Right: Kayaking is just one of the many activities guests can partake in. This page, left: Sweeping balconies make the ultimate viewing deck. Above: With hundreds of kilometers of steep cliffs, glacial valleys, and rain forests, the rugged coastal landscape is just one aspect of the diverse topography.

Above: The creative architecture of the main lodge building is simple yet complex. The long horizontal lines mimic the ocean horizon.
Right: With 29 kilometers (18 miles) of seafront, the area has plenty of sheltered coves for surfing.

are situated on 35 hectares (84 acres) of private property on the northeastern corner of Tasmania, and provide accommodation for twenty guests. In an effort to minimize the impact on the earth, guests are called upon to pump their own water for showers. (They last four minutes.) Further, all sewage and organic kitchen waste is treated on-site in a Clivus Multrum dry composting system. All this, in the name of environmental progress and enlightened living. The Bay of Fires Lodge is home to over one hundred species of wildlife—including eastern gray kangaroos, echidnas, brushtail possums, wombats, wallabies, and, yes, Tasmanian devils. And chances are, the less negative the impact made on the land, its inhabitants, and its resources, the more positive the impact all around.

CUISINE: The walk guides are multitaskers and prepare all the meals. Dinners at the lodge begin with local wine, cheese, and crackers by the fireplace, followed by a communal seated meal, which is mostly organic.

ACTIVITIES: The most spectacular reason for visiting Bay of Fires Lodge lies in the very act of getting there: the hike to the lodge. Striking in its seclusion and breathtakingly beautiful, the path winds down rocky coves and endless white beaches, inspiring moments of individual contemplation. The Bay of Fires Lodge buildings are the only structures on a 20 kilometer (13 mile) stretch of pristine coastal wilderness. Other activities include surfing, canoeing, and swimming.

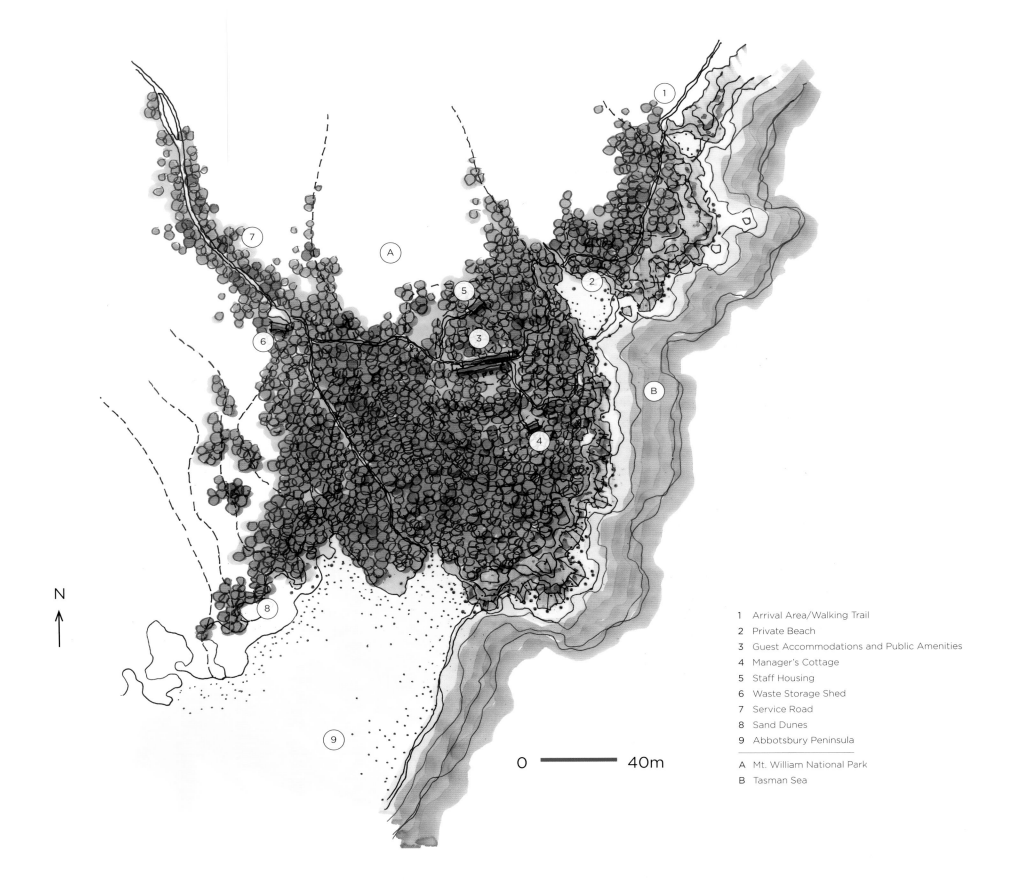

N

1   Arrival Area/Walking Trail

2   Private Beach

3   Guest Accommodations and Public Amenities

4   Manager's Cottage

5   Staff Housing

6   Waste Storage Shed

7   Service Road

8   Sand Dunes

9   Abbotsbury Peninsula

A   Mt. William National Park

B   Tasman Sea

0   40m

CHUMBE ISLAND ECOLODGE

CHUMBE ISLAND, TANZANIA

DATE COMPLETED
1998

OWNER
Sibylle Riedmiller (Germany)

ARCHITECTS
Georg Fiebig (Australia)
Jan Hülsemann (Germany)
Professor Per Krusche (Germany)

Thousands of miles from the Great Barrier Reef and even farther from the turquoise colored marine reserves of the Caribbean lies Chumbe Island Coral Park, a remote coral-fringed getaway off the east coast of Africa and just south of Zanzibar Island. Though perhaps lesser known than the traditional luxury destinations of Brampton Island and Parrot Cay, Chumbe Island rivals its tropical counterparts both in terms of its scenic beauty and its idyllic atmosphere. Designated as Tanzania's first managed marine-protected area in 1994, Chumbe Island has earned a reputation as one of the world's most diverse reefs, home to almost four hundred species of fish and two hundred species of hard coral. Over 90 percent of Chumbe Island is covered by a pristine "coral rag" forest, which is inhabited by two endangered faunal species: the coconut crab and Ader's duiker (a small forest-dwelling antelope). As if these weren't heady enough qualifications to make it a modern-day paradise, Chumbe Island is also host to Chumbe Island Ecolodge, one of the most authentic ecolodges in the world.

The brainchild of Sibylle Riedmiller, a German conservationist who came to the area in the 1980s to manage education projects, Chumbe Ecolodge scores high for its strict adherence to the main principles of ecolodges—conservation, local community benefits, and interpretation. As the accommodation component of Chumbe Island Coral Park, the ecolodge is instilled with a rare sense of ownership and environmental responsibility. Former fishermen were hired as park rangers to bring conservation to the community, and many other locals work in a number of employment capacities. Chumbe also hires women, a remarkable practice given the fact that the local Islamic culture discourages them from working; even where employment is found, opportunities for advancement in the workplace are limited. Not so at Chumbe. In addition to the supportive staff environment, Chumbe also fosters a nurturing educational component, the Chumbe Education Program. This vital series of classes sponsors local school visits to the island and teacher-training workshops, all

Previous spread: The lodge in situ, overlooking the tropical waters of the Zanzibar Channel. Opposite page, clockwise from top left: Each bungalow is decorated with handmade furniture, constructed from local materials; Guests enjoying a drink at the cozy outdoor, sunset-facing lounge; Guest Bungalow, seen against the backdrop of the Chumbe Lighthouse; Guests' arrival experience begins at the exotic island of Zanzibar with its narrow pedestrian-only streets and rich Islamic cultures; Mouthwatering dishes and snacks include a mixture of Zanzibarian, Arabic, Indian, and African delicacies.

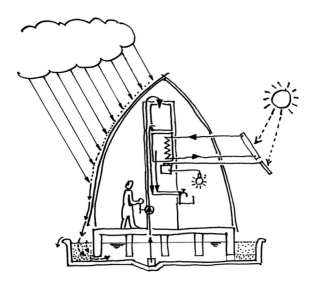 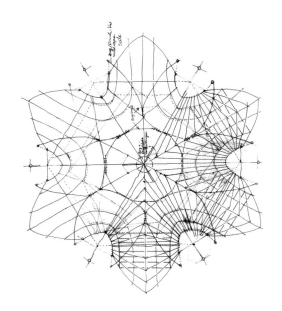 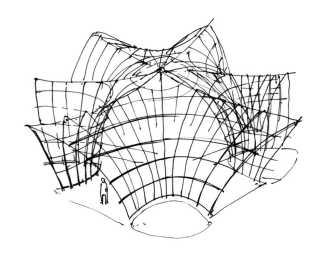

This page, left: Schematic of the eco-shower and filtration system. Captured rainwater passes though a complex filtration system and is stored in spacious underground cisterns (under each bungalow). Water is hand-pumped through a solar-powered heating system for bathroom use. Center: Complex roof plan of the main lodge building. Right: Axonometric of the structure of the main lodge building. Opposite, left: The spiral effect of the interior of the 100-year-old Chumbe Lighthouse. Right: The open-air, no-doors, no-windows design of the bungalows allow for a form of natural air conditioning.

geared toward building environmental awareness and ensuring that Chumbe Ecolodge rolls out the green carpet like no other.

The innovatively creative design of Chumbe Ecolodge was the result of a unique collaboration of three architects (Professor Per Krusche, George Fiebig, and Jan Hülsemann) and conservationist/developer Sibylle Riedmiller. Each of the lodge's seven bungalows is a self-sustaining unit that utilizes creative architectural design and a flair for the romantic. Decorated with Tanzanian art, colorful fabrics, and handmade furniture, and graced with views of the sea, the bungalows are truly a honeymooner's delight. Outfitted with thatched, palm frond roofs and featuring an open-air design that uses sea breezes as a natural form of air-conditioning, each bungalow is designed to blend harmoniously with its surroundings. The lodge's rooftop rainwater-collection system and solar-powered lights are just a small sampling of the "green friendly" architecture. Also in play are dry composting toilets to conserve water, plant beds that utilize gray water, and flashlights powered by photovoltaic (PV) cells that eliminate the need for batteries.

With its marine conservation, educational program, and innovative ecotechnology, the multi-award-winning Chumbe Ecolodge isn't the typical all-inclusive, which is a good thing. Not only can guests luxuriate in the scenic East African setting, they can also rest assured that they are giving something back to the community that's hosted them.

CUISINE: Chefs serve local produce in an array of Zanzibari, Indian, and Arabic dishes in the former lighthouse keeper's home, which has been remodeled into a giant clam-shaped dining bungalow.

ACTIVITIES: Since all of Chumbe Island is a nature reserve, there is no end to the activities guests can enjoy. Whether snorkeling through the reef sanctuary, traversing the nature trails in the forest reserve, or soaking in the breathtaking views from atop the historical Chumbe Lighthouse, Chumbe Ecolodge has something for everyone.

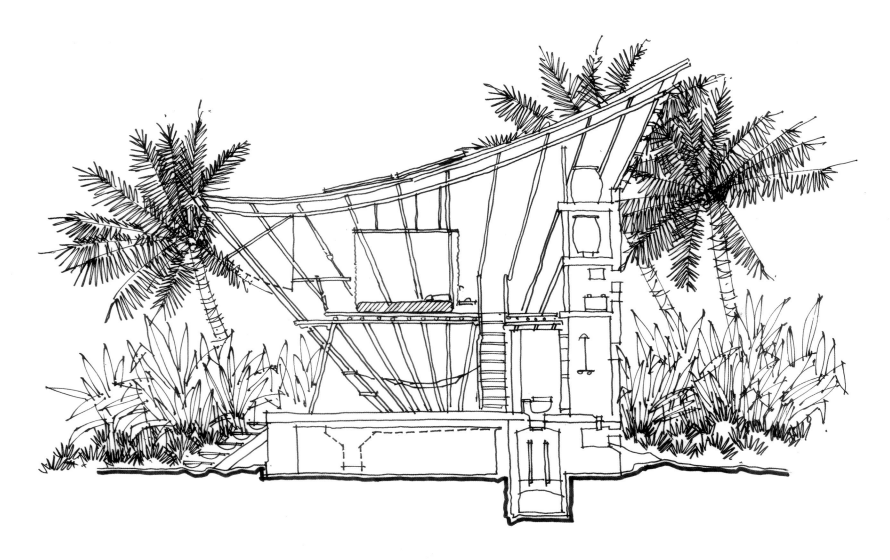

Above: A cross-section of the Guest Bungalow demonstrates the intricacies of the sewage system. Each bungalow is equipped with composting toilets, which prevent sewage from seeping into the Reef Sanctuary. Wind-powered vent pipes and gradient storage replicate the experience of using a regular toilet. Bottom, left: The influence of the Chumbe Island Coral Park is seen in the rooms' décor, which prominently reflect the area's protected fish, coral, turtles, and other species. Bottom, right: A couple enjoys a romantic Swahili dinner in the renovated lighthouse.

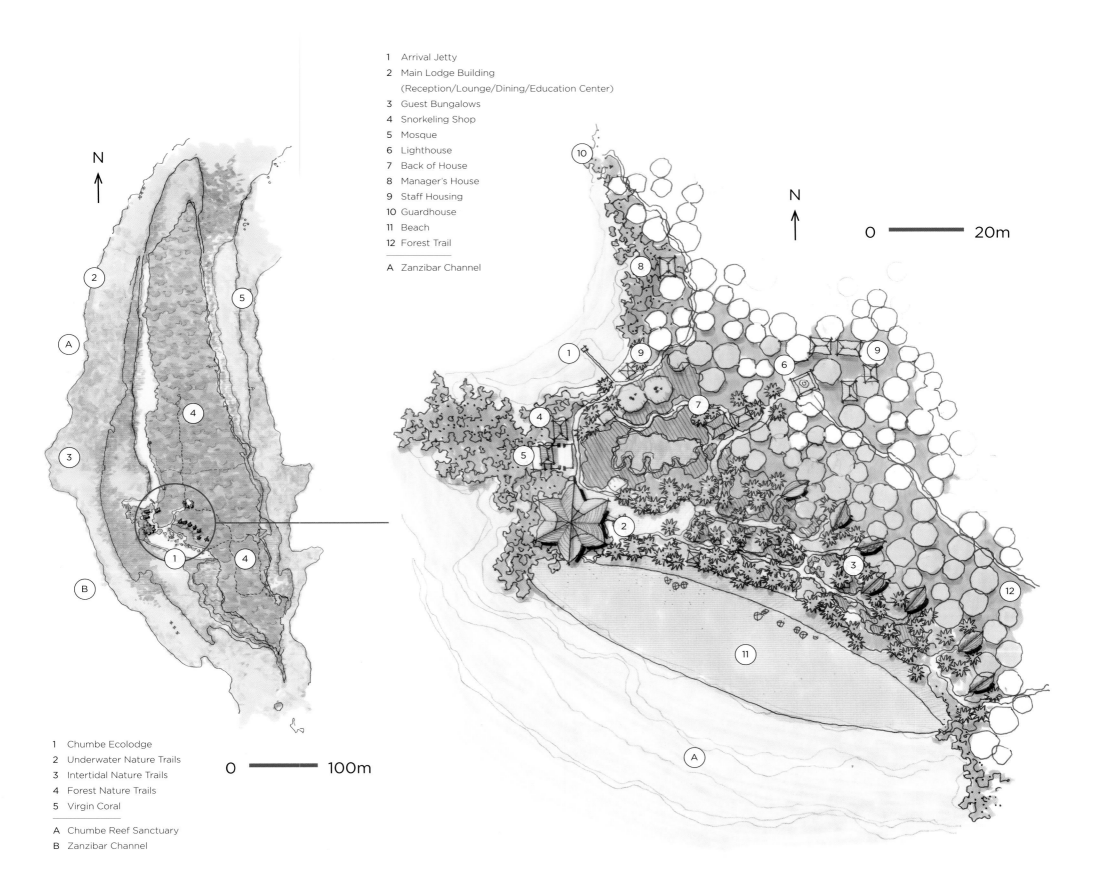

1 Arrival Jetty
2 Main Lodge Building
  (Reception/Lounge/Dining/Education Center)
3 Guest Bungalows
4 Snorkeling Shop
5 Mosque
6 Lighthouse
7 Back of House
8 Manager's House
9 Staff Housing
10 Guardhouse
11 Beach
12 Forest Trail

A Zanzibar Channel

1 Chumbe Ecolodge
2 Underwater Nature Trails
3 Intertidal Nature Trails
4 Forest Nature Trails
5 Virgin Coral

A Chumbe Reef Sanctuary
B Zanzibar Channel

N

0 ▬▬▬ 100m

N

0 ▬▬▬ 20m

COMMUNITY OWNED AND OPERATED

One of the biggest trends in ecotourism today is community owned and operated lodges. Vital to these lodges' success is the empowerment, integration, and participation of indigenous communities and international support. The three ecolodges presented in this chapter are not only leaders in their field, in terms of ownership, hiring local community members, and creating comprehensive integration programs, but they are also top-notch in terms of their facilities, service, food, and amenities. More important, however, they exemplify a simple idea: An ecolodge can only be as successful as the people who own and operate it.

A small body of determined spirits fired by an unquenchable faith in their mission can alter the course of history.
—Mahatma Ghandi

CREE VILLAGE ECOLODGE

NORTHERN ONTARIO, CANADA

DATE COMPLETED
2000

OWNER
MoCreebec Council of the Cree Nation

ARCHITECT
Clive Levitt (Canada)

Surrounded by the rugged beauty of the Canadian subarctic, Cree Village Ecolodge is located on Moose Factory Island along the Moose River. It is the first aboriginal owned and operated authentic ecolodge in Canada and the United States. The visionary of the ecolodge, Randy Kapashesit, also happens to be the chief of the MoCreebec Council of the Cree Nation (approximately five hundred members). Since opening its doors in 2001, Cree Village has emerged as one of the most contextual environmentally and socially friendly lodges on the North American continent, thanks in no small part to its comprehensive energy conservation efforts, locally employed staff, and innovative design.

The ecolodge has two main goals: to live lightly on the earth and to share its profits with every member of the MoCreebec community. Greg Williams, lodge manager, explains that living lightly "means that every detail, from the exterior building materials ... to the interior furnishings, maximizes the use of natural products ... We minimize the use

of synthetics. Even the paint and carpets are nontoxic." In an effort to remain true to traditional Native American values while focusing on cultural and ecological sustainability, the lodge architecturally references its Cree history while using modern, ecofriendly technologies, like its no-flush, no-water composting toilets, low-e argon windows, energy-efficient light fittings, low-noise ceiling fans (the lodge has no air-conditioning), and recycled rubber stairway floors. Committed to fulfilling its second goal, the lodge is working toward economic sustainability, too.

The architectural approach is that of "continuity of the vernacular." Modeled on a traditional Cree *shaapuhtuwaan*, meaning "long teepee with doors at each end," the lodge's restaurant overlooks the picturesque Moose River. Traditionally, the shaapuhtuwaan consisted of two teepees linked by a lean-to, with the whole covered in deerskin or moss. Cree Village Ecolodge's version of the shaapuhtuwaan features a vaulted, cathedral-like ceiling, cedar interiors,

Previous spread: The lodge in situ, bathed by the lights of aurora borealis and surrounded by the rugged beauty of the Canadian subarctic. Opposite: The teepee-inspired gift shop. The conference center is in the background. This page: The ecolodge is considered one of the most environmentally advanced accommodations in Canada. Windows and doors face north to take advantage of natural wind patterns, as the facility has no standard air conditioning system. Instead, high-efficient, low-noise ceiling fans are used.

Above: Guests at the lodge can experience an authentic Cree *shaapuhtuwaan* by visiting a local villager's home. Right: The lodge combines the old-world values and traditions of the MoCreebec people, with a twenty-first century architectural application.

and 14.5m (48 foot) tall poles of lodgepole pine mounted in place by an intricate hinge system. The great room is a modern-day interpretation of the Cree gathering place, where multiple families would share the space for living, eating, and storytelling. Today, guests gather around the limestone fireplace—the tiles of which are embedded with animal footprints—to swap tales from the day's various ecotourism activities. The gift shop, located in the "xeroscape" garden, is a reinterpretation of the wigwam.

Building large-scale accommodation in the Arctic is no easy task, given the weather restrictions. Timing and scheduling had to be precise: Supplies and equipment were delivered first by truck or rail to Cochrane, then by rail to Moosonee, and finally to Moose Factory Island. The lodge itself features twenty rooms, all of which are named after animals indigenous to the area. The first-floor rooms, for example, are named in honor of the *amiskw* (beaver) and *waapush* (rabbit), while the second floor is home to such room names as *michisuuch* (bald eagle) and *wapihyou* (ptarmigan). These calling cards serve as a gentle reminder of the Cree's generations-long connection with the land's original inhabitants. A tour of the lodge's property, led by the owners themselves, further reveals this symbiotic relationship and gives guests a glimpse into the genuine Cree way of life.

CUISINE: During the summer and fall seasons, the restaurant offers traditional aboriginal cuisine and menu items that have been selected to pay tribute to the traditions of the Cree people. Throughout the year, natural menu items, such as wild rice and pure maple syrup, are used that support other indigenous communities in their sustainable food productions. Organically grown, fair-trade coffee is also served, which helps cooperatives in Mexico. The restaurant provides a healthier alternative to the local population who frequent the lodge and mingle with guests.

ACTIVITIES: Lodge staff and local operators provide extensive ecotours and excursions around the surrounding wilderness. Guests can kayak or canoe across the Moose River to bird-watch at the bird sanctuary on nearby Shipstead Island; dig for fossils in the shale on the river's shore; snowshoe at the edge of James Bay; cross-country ski at Tidewater Provincial Park; hike around Moose Factory Island; and learn about fur traders in the island's Centennial Park Museum. For those guests craving more relaxation than adventure, there are beluga whale– and seal-watching river tours, and the rare opportunity to see the northern lights of aurora borealis.

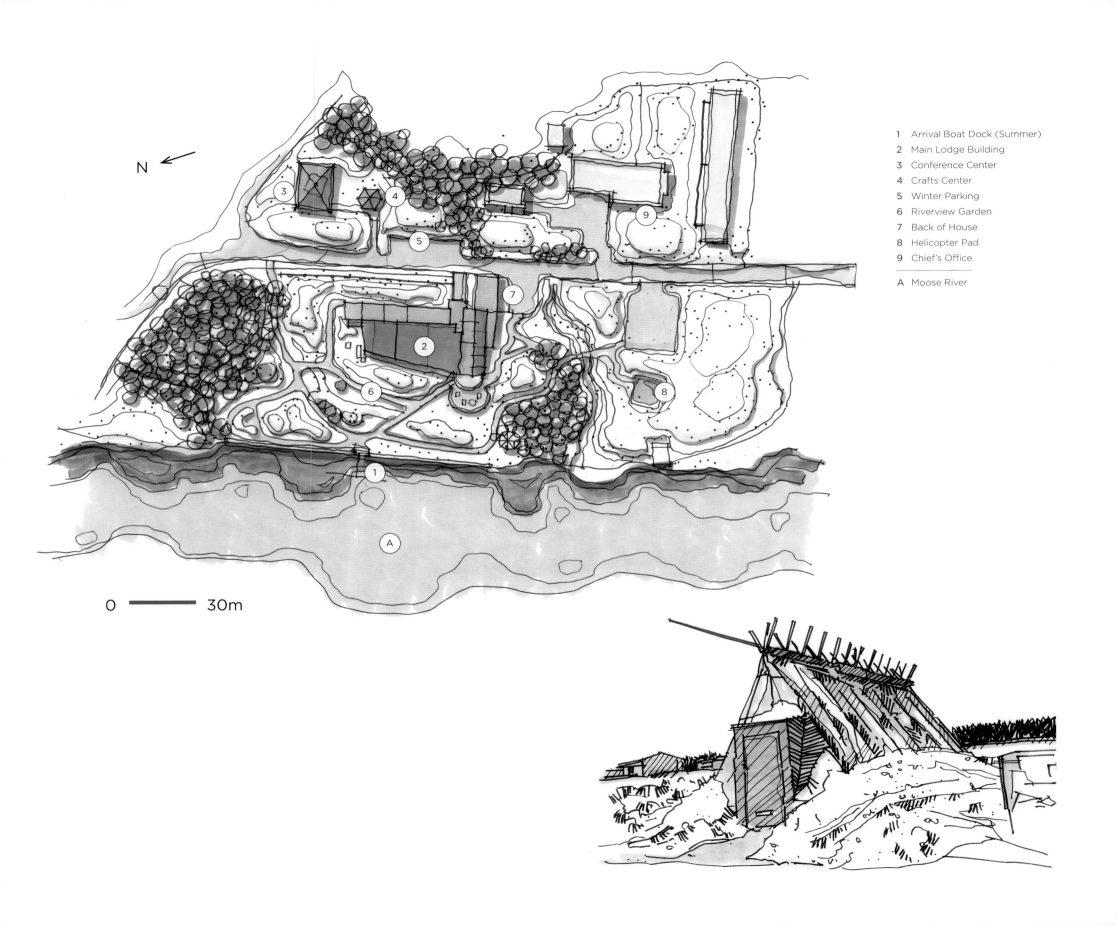

N

1 Arrival Boat Dock (Summer)
2 Main Lodge Building
3 Conference Center
4 Crafts Center
5 Winter Parking
6 Riverview Garden
7 Back of House
8 Helicopter Pad
9 Chief's Office

A Moose River

0 ——— 30m

CHALALÁN ECOLODGE

MADIDI NATIONAL PARK, BOLIVIA

DATE COMPLETED
1998

OWNER
Community of San José de Uchupiamonas

MASTER PLANNER
Design Workshop (United States)

ARCHITECT
James K (Bolivia)

Chalalán Ecolodge is located in the Amazon Basin in the heart of the Madidi National Park, which has long been considered a tropical Andean hotspot with the highest biodiversity of endemic plants on the planet (some forty-five thousand plant species and one thousand tropical bird species). Buffered by the shores of the Chalalán Lagoon, the lodge is more than an exotic accommodation by the water. It is the culmination of six years of hard work by the people of San José de Uchupiamonas and two foreign aid organizations, dedicated to supporting the community's initiative to save itself from poverty, government disinterest, and struggling social services. Ecotourism, in this sense, provided a very real lifeline, both financially and socially, to members of the San José de Uchupiamonas. The community now has the titles to its land, clean drinking water, and health and education services. By generating direct and indirect benefits to the local community, and supporting the well-being of future generations, Chalalán epitomizes the genuine community owned and operated ecolodge.

Seventy-four families helped build the thirty-three-bed lodge, with each family contributing a minimum of seventy days' worth of labor. Designed to resemble the traditional Tacana-style cabins and using environmentally friendly materials—the chonta palm (*Iriartea deltoidea*) for the walls and jatata palm leaves (*Geonoma deversa*) for the roof—the lodge uses solar power and a liquid waste-treatment system, which combines the effect of the sun and biological processes to guarantee a minimum impact on the surrounding environment. In an effort to make the most positive impact on the lives of the local and international communities, Chalalán provides environmental education programs that stress the importance of preserving the natural heritage. During the tourist season, the lodge offers thirty-seven direct employment opportunities to the local community, furthering self-sustainability. Within ten years' time, it is the lodge's hope to be a highly competitive community business, with an ear bent toward fighting poverty and social inequality.

Previous spread: The lodge in situ, on the shores of Chalalán Lagoon, Madidi National Park. Opposite: The ecolodge is built using material indigenous to the area: Walls are made from the chonta palm (*Iriartea deltoidea*) and covered with matting; the roofs are woven with jatata palm leaves (*Geonoma deversa*); and the floors are made of fine hardwood. This page, left and right, top: The ecolodge is both simple in style yet decidedly exotic in nature. Right, bottom: This tropical area is home to 45,000 different plant species and thousands of birds and amphibians, like this tree frog.

Above: The Chalalán restaurant, complete with traditional thatched leaved ceilings, can seat up to forty people. Right: A traditional clay oven is used to prepare native dishes.

Secluded deep within the jungle, Chalalán is accessible only by boat up the Beni and Tuichi rivers. With its strong moral compass pointed in the right direction, Chalalán not only leads guests to drier ground, but it also leads them to a more enriched way of living.

CUISINE: The Chalalán restaurant offers local, national, and international dishes. A traditional clay oven is used to prepare native dishes like baked plantain and potatoes, and meals are accompanied by the season's fruit juices. The professionally equipped kitchen can also accommodate vegans and those with special dietary requirements.

ACTIVITIES: The local Quechua guide provides tours through 30 kilometers (19 miles) of trails in Madidi National Park, some of the most pristine land on earth. The lagoon is an ideal habitat for monkeys, caimans, turtles, tapirs, and macaws, and reverberates with a continuous symphony of birdsong punctuated by shouts of howler monkeys, particularly at dawn and dusk. Back at the lodge, guests can learn about traditional crafts, farming techniques, and food. Evenings are filled with story time, during which locals engage guests with accounts of the community's history, customs, and beliefs. This is followed with traditional Quecha-Tacana music and dancing.

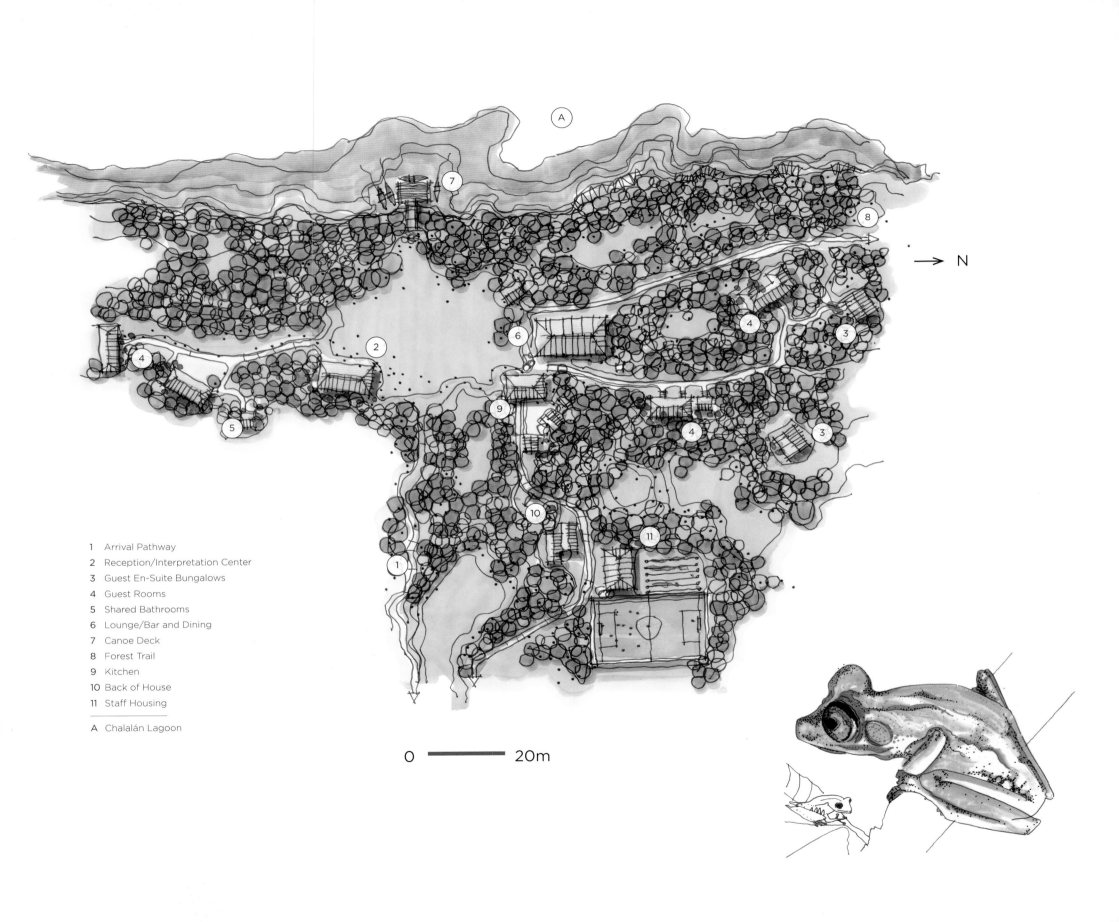

1   Arrival Pathway
2   Reception/Interpretation Center
3   Guest En-Suite Bungalows
4   Guest Rooms
5   Shared Bathrooms
6   Lounge/Bar and Dining
7   Canoe Deck
8   Forest Trail
9   Kitchen
10 Back of House
11 Staff Housing

A   Chalalán Lagoon

0 ———— 20m

N

IL NGWESI LODGE
LAIKIPIA, KENYA

DATE COMPLETED
1996

OWNER
Il Ngwesi Community

DESIGNERS
Simon du Fresne and Michael Dyer

Adjacent to the Ngare Ndare River on the edge of the Mukogodo Hills, Il Ngwesi Lodge offers sweeping panoramic views across northern Kenya, a land where low plains rise to central highlands, and signature African wildlife species—elephant, lion, leopard, buffalo, cheetah, and wild dog—roam freely. The lodge was created with the assistance of Lewa Wildlife Conservancy and by using grant funds from United States Agency for International Development—USAID. It is owned by the Il Ngwesi community of the Mukogodo division of Laikipia district, and is Africa's first community owned and operated ecolodge.

Previous to the creation of Il Ngwesi Lodge, the area was undeveloped with little economic activity, except for subsistence pastoralism. The lodge has provided countless job opportunities for the locals and has helped them move toward financial self-sufficiency. Everything about the lodge—from decisions about where to build to the quality of building material used in final construction to basic managerial

systems—has been the result of a collaborative effort by the Il Ngwesi community, who have now taken over the marketing of the lodge as well.

Comprised of six individual *bandas* (cottages), all of which have adjoining open-air showers, Il Ngwesi is designed to reflect and preserve its connection to the surrounding landscape. As such, the majority of the construction materials are from the local region: The roof is made from local grass; the walls are built with a mixture of sand, soil, cement, and wire mesh; rafters are made from cedar from the nearby Mukogodo Forest; and the walls' beams are made from Lowveld newtonia (*Newtonia hildebrantii*), which is so strong that elephants cannot break it. Timber columns were harvested as deadwood while other timber came from plantations.

Il Ngwesi Lodge has to be one of the most exemplary examples of deadwood architecture in the world. The lodge was constructed of select pieces of fallen timber found on

Previous spread: The lodge in situ, set up on a promontory of the Il Ngwesi group ranch. With its "open-to-the-bush" design, guests can view wildlife direct from their rooms. Opposite page, clockwise from top left: The ecolodge is known for its open design and stunning panoramic views. The infinity pool is a guest favorite; Constructed from local materials, the ecolodge features innovative design elements that make it a stand out; One of the main reasons that Il Ngwesi Ecolodge was developed was to protect elephant migratory routes; Old-world Maasai Moran meets new-world technology. This page: The *bandas* (guest cottages), mostly built by natural materials, blend harmoniously into the landscape.

Above: The thatched pavilion and full moon cast their reflections on the infinity pool. Right: The Honeymoon Suite and Room Five each have a large four-poster double bed. The bed has wheels and can be rolled out for a night under the stars. Opposite: The boulder-like look of the Il Ngwesi cottages in the foreground seemingly blend into the surrounding rock cliffs.

the forest floor, which have been brought to life through the sheer creativity of designer and builder Simon du Fresne. The organic and sculptural deadwood has been used for columns, balusters, toilet-roll holders, tabletops, handrails, step risers, furniture supports, etc.

Il Ngwesi Lodge is unique in the sense that there are no doors or windows in any of the bandas. The bandas' front walls, including that of the toilet, are a meter (just over 3 feet) high to allow cool breezes and dramatic vistas of the ranch's 6,875 hectares (16,500 acres) and the Maroroi Hills. Lighting is solar, and water—gravity fed from a spring—is used wisely. An infinity swimming pool—run on a solar pump and nestled in the surrounding wilderness—provides a truly luxurious touch to Il Ngwesi Lodge's otherwise simple setting.

A percentage of the revenue generated by the lodge is distributed back to the community via a number of conservation programs dedicated to maintaining local schools, bursaries, veterinary and health facilities, and antipoaching

initiatives. Because of the Il Ngwesi Lodge's efforts, wildlife is regaining a presence in the area, the community itself is becoming self-sufficient, and visitors the world over are given the opportunity to experience for themselves a place of refuge and solitude unlike anywhere else.

CUISINE: Many of the vegetables and fruits are grown on an organic farm located at the edge of the ranch. Traditional and international meals are served either at the main dining hall, by the swimming pool, or in the bandas.

ACTIVITIES: Guests can visit the authentic Maasai Cultural Manyatta (homestead) where they can learn about traditional Maasai practices or explore the area by foot or by camel following the Ngare Ndare River with local guides. Game drives and walks are also an excellent way to see the lay of the land.

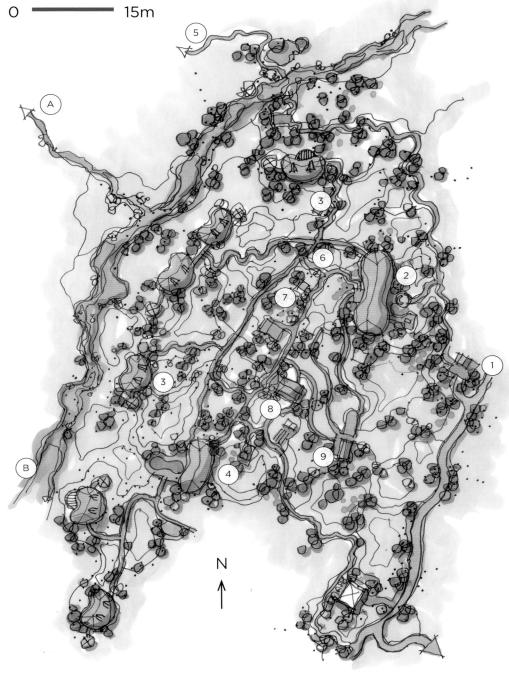

O ▬▬▬▬▬ 15m

N

1   Arrival Car Park
2   Main Lodge Building
3   Guest Bandas (Cottages)
4   Swimming Pool and Pavilion
5   Waterfall Trail
6   Administrative Offices
7   Kitchen
8   Back of House
9   Senior Staff Housing

A   Maroroi Hill
B   Yiari River (Seasonal)

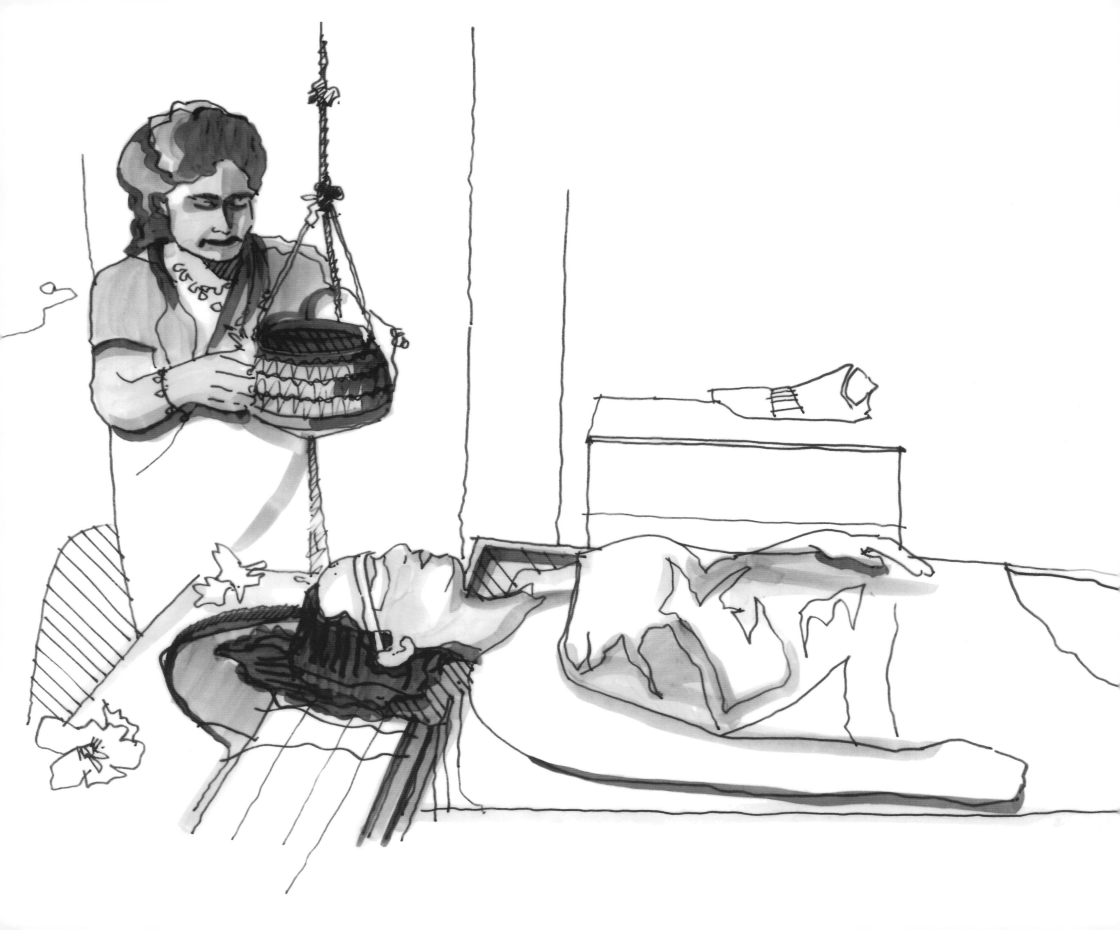

HOLISTIC WELLNESS PROGRAMS

Holistic wellness programs are growing in popularity all over the world, especially in the realm of ecotourism. Usually low-impact, these alternative programs offer a holistic blend of physical, mental, and spiritual activities, all designed to encourage a healthy state of well-being. While most programs provide detoxification activities for the mind and body—reiki, tai-chi, yoga, ayurveda, and indigenous massage treatments, for example—some go one step further, creating individual treatment and diet programs that last one to three weeks. The ecolodges presented here feature expert staff who are knowledgeable in the latest wellness trends and techniques, as well as a comprehensive host of products, services, and activities guaranteed to deliver transformative life experiences.

When we heal the earth,
we heal ourselves.
—David Orr

RANWELI HOLIDAY VILLAGE

WAIKKAL, SRI LANKA

DATE REMODELED
1996

OWNER
Ranweli Holiday Village Ltd.

ARCHITECTS
Mihindu Keerthiratne Associates Ltd. (Sri Lanka)

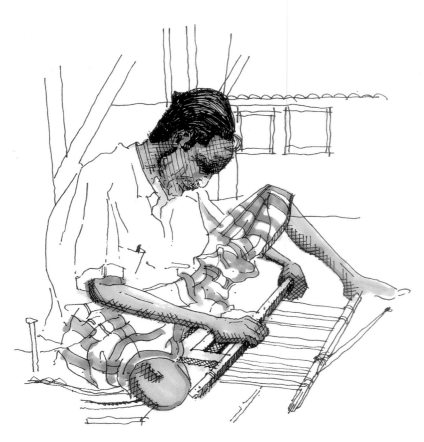

Ranweli Holiday Village is located on the western coast of Sri Lanka and stands within a 9 hectare (22 acre) peninsula bordered by a wide, sandy beach on one side and winding rivers and mangrove forests on the other. Nestled between these habitats are rows of coconut trees and, beneath them, a steady string of clay-roof-tiled bungalows. Ranweli is an extreme makeover project. From a traditional mass-tourism hotel built in 1975, it was remodeled into a full-fledged ecolodge by the late Chandra de Silva, then director of Ranweli. For each bungalow built at Ranweli, only one coconut tree was removed, and the trunks were used to create the walkway pillars. These covered interlocking walkways connect the bungalows and lead guests toward the center of the hotel village, bypassing tended palm gardens along the way. Blending the traditions of the indigenous Sri Lankan culture with Western architectural design, Ranweli offers a serene retreat from the everyday.

Ranweli excels in nearly every arena of ecoconservationism by following a dedicated four-pronged tenet: 1) minimizing environmental impact 2) promoting environmental and cultural education 3) supporting preservation efforts, and 4) supporting programs and efforts that benefit the local community. From the solar-powered showers to the environmental education meetings to the in-room environmental guidebook to the weekly artisan programs (whereby local artists teach their crafts to guests), Ranweli puts its philosophical tenets into practice. As if this weren't enough, Ranweli goes one step further in establishing itself as a place of holistic wellness. It promotes Ayurveda, which is India's ancient science of healing, combining medicine, therapy, and massage to produce wellness in the mind, body, and spirit without any side effects. Ranweli's comprehensive wellness programs—the Ayurvedic Center managed by qualified doctors, a menu of exercise, dietary, and meditation options, and an organic herb garden—transforms Ranweli into a transcendent experience.

Long considered the "science of life" in Indian culture, Ayurveda focuses on preventative measures to restore

Previous spread: The lodge in situ, on a peninsula in western Sri Lanka. Opposite: The retail village is laid out around a brick fountain and is a blend of Western and Eastern aesthetic sensibilities.

balance to the body, spiritual well-being, and wholeness to life. Ranweli's Ayurvedic Center offers both health and beauty therapies for a range of treatments, all designed to bring the body to a place of wellness, relaxation, and health. Rounding out the Center are an impressive array of yoga classes—guaranteed to satisfy both novice and professional—meditation programs, and the organic herb garden, which consists of over one hundred plants, all used in Ayurvedic treatments. Sri Lanka is affectionately known

as the "enchanted one." Whether guests stay for one week, one day, or one hour, it is they who feel enchanted at the end of their visit.

CUISINE: Whenever possible, fresh produce is procured from the local community and some of the vegetables come from the on-site organic vegetable plots. Ranweli provides guests with several unique dining experiences. The vegetarian Ayurvedic restaurant has a spectacular view of the Indian

Opposite, clockwise from top left: The land was originally a coconut plantation surrounded by mangroves and screw pines (*Pandanus odoratissimus*), which today provide a meditative enclosure for guest activities; Unique experiences include dining in a secluded mangrove forest environment; Bedroom of a typical bungalow. Décor includes terra-cotta pots, brass lamps, and artwork by local craftsmen; Connecting walkways lead to the heart of the mangrove community. This page: From the lobby of the Ayurvedic Center, seen here, to the rooms themselves, every detail of the ecolodge is meant to inspire relaxation.

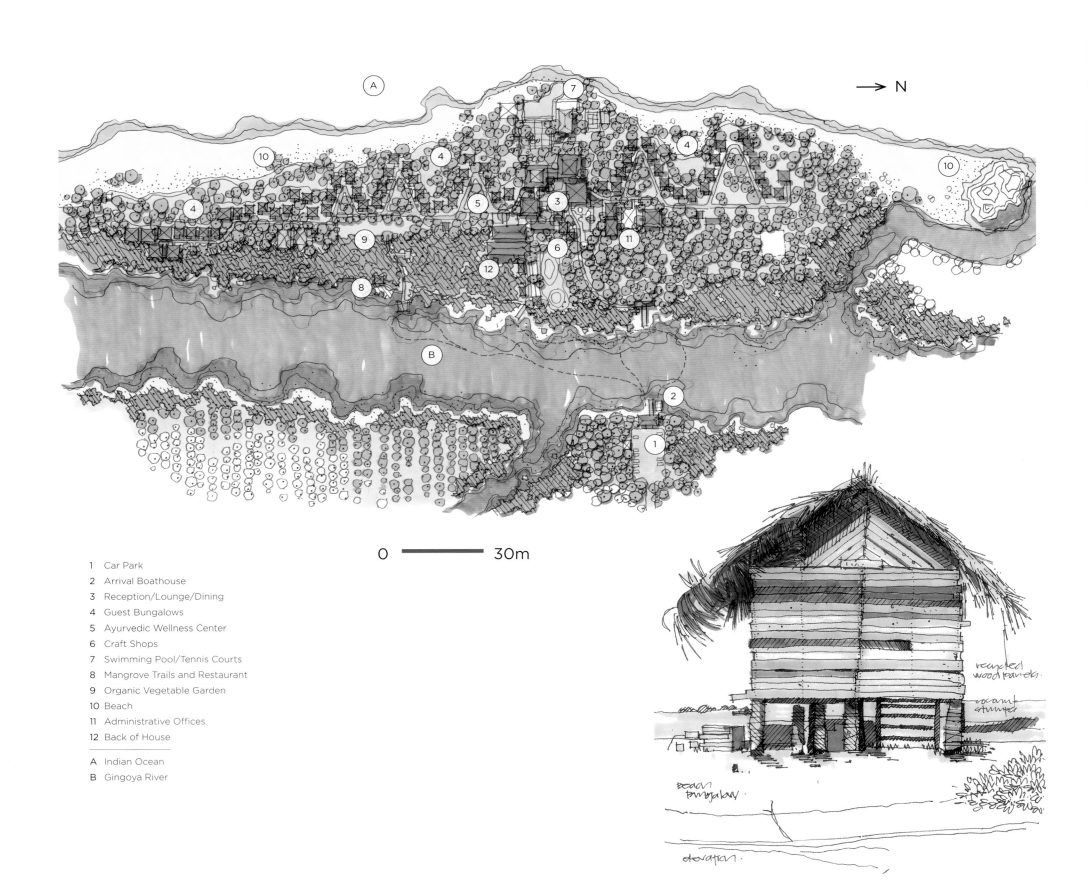

→ N

1   Car Park
2   Arrival Boathouse
3   Reception/Lounge/Dining
4   Guest Bungalows
5   Ayurvedic Wellness Center
6   Craft Shops
7   Swimming Pool/Tennis Courts
8   Mangrove Trails and Restaurant
9   Organic Vegetable Garden
10 Beach
11 Administrative Offices
12 Back of House

A Indian Ocean
B Gingoya River

0   30m

recycled
wood panels

coconut
stumps

beach
bungalow

elevation

Ocean, while the mangrove restaurant overlooks the river. A romantic dinner cruise is attended by a personal butler, a chef, and a ferryman, and is designed to meet all the guests' dining needs, from low-sodium, low-calorie entrees to more exotic fare. A small fruit stall called the Palathuru Masse is located next to the main bar and serves fresh fruit juices and herbal drinks of medicinal value.

ACTIVITIES: Explore the unique ecosystem around the mangroves and the 1,250 hectare (3,000 acre) Wildlife Sanctuary of Anaivilundawa, which is home to approximately fifty different bird species and two wetland areas. Bird-watch on the river by boat, partake in nature walks with a trained naturalist along the Ranweli trail, take a bicycle tour through the lush countryside, or kayak along the waterways. As a scenic glimpse into local Sri Lankan flora and fauna, it doesn't get much better than this.

Left: Traditional fishing huts of the Gingoya River are located adjacent to Ranweli. Above, top: Sri Lanka has the greatest density of biodiversity of any other country in Asia. A kingfisher waiting for a kill. Above, bottom: Flowers adorn the lodge, creating a feeling of tranquility.

THE LODGE AT CHAA CREEK

CAYO DISTRICT, BELIZE

DATE COMPLETED
1981

OWNERS
Mick and Lucy Fleming

SUSTAINABLE TOURISM PLANNER
HM Design (United States)

LANDSCAPE ARCHITECTS (MASTER PLAN)
HM Design (United States) and
40 North (Costa Rica)

ARCHITECTS (COTTAGES)
Hedel Gongora Santa Maria

INTERIOR DESIGN
Brendan O'Donaghue

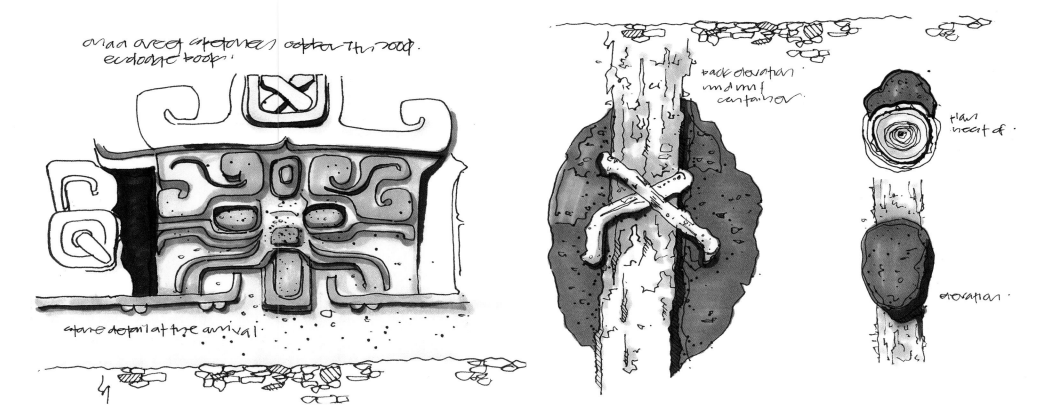

As a private 147 hectare (365 acre) nature reserve set along the banks of the Macal River in the foothills of the Maya Mountains, Chaa Creek resembles a grand colonial estate with its manicured gardens and liveried staff. One could be forgiven for being swayed by its outward appearance, which is lush in vegetation and graced with scenic views and inspired architecture. The luxurious surroundings, however, belie a founding commitment to the core principles of ecotourism and a back-to-the-land sensibility. Owners Mick and Lucy Fleming discovered the land in 1977 when it was a simple yet very overgrown 58 hectare (140 acre) farm in the Cayo District. Over the course of several years, this simple farm grew into what is today known as Chaa Creek, complete with luxury villas, a spa, natural history center, over seventy Mayan archaeological sites, hiking, medicinal, and horseback-riding trails, several conservation and educational programs, and the Chaa Creek Inland Expedition program, which specializes in ecoadventure tourism.

A vital part of Chaa Creek is the Macal River Camp, a compound of ten wood-and-canvas cottages with no electricity that give guests the opportunity to experience Belize without modern-day distraction. For those guests who crave more luxury in their accommodations, there are twenty-three palm-thatched cottage rooms, including garden suites with Jacuzzis, built amid fig and quamwood trees and overlooking the Macal River. Chaa Creek was one of the first ecolodges in the world to introduce the "wellness" experience to its guests. The Spa at Chaa Creek is the brainchild of the owners' daughter. It overlooks the Macal River Valley and provides guests with a full-service spa package, which includes aromatherapy treatments, herbal massage therapies, and seaweed body wraps, among other amenities.

Throughout the years, the Flemings have dedicated themselves to creating a model of low-impact, sustainable development while stimulating interest in the environment, natural history, and local culture. This guiding principle is

Previous spread: The lodge in situ, deep in the Mayan rain forests of Belize. Opposite page, clockwise from top left: The spa features specialized therapists trained in the latest wellness techniques and practices; View of the ecolodge's horse stable; The Mayan-inspired organic garden supplies the kitchen with most of the vegetables; The Spa at Chaa Creek, surrounded by a canopy of lush greenery; Lounge and study area for one of the luxury villas.

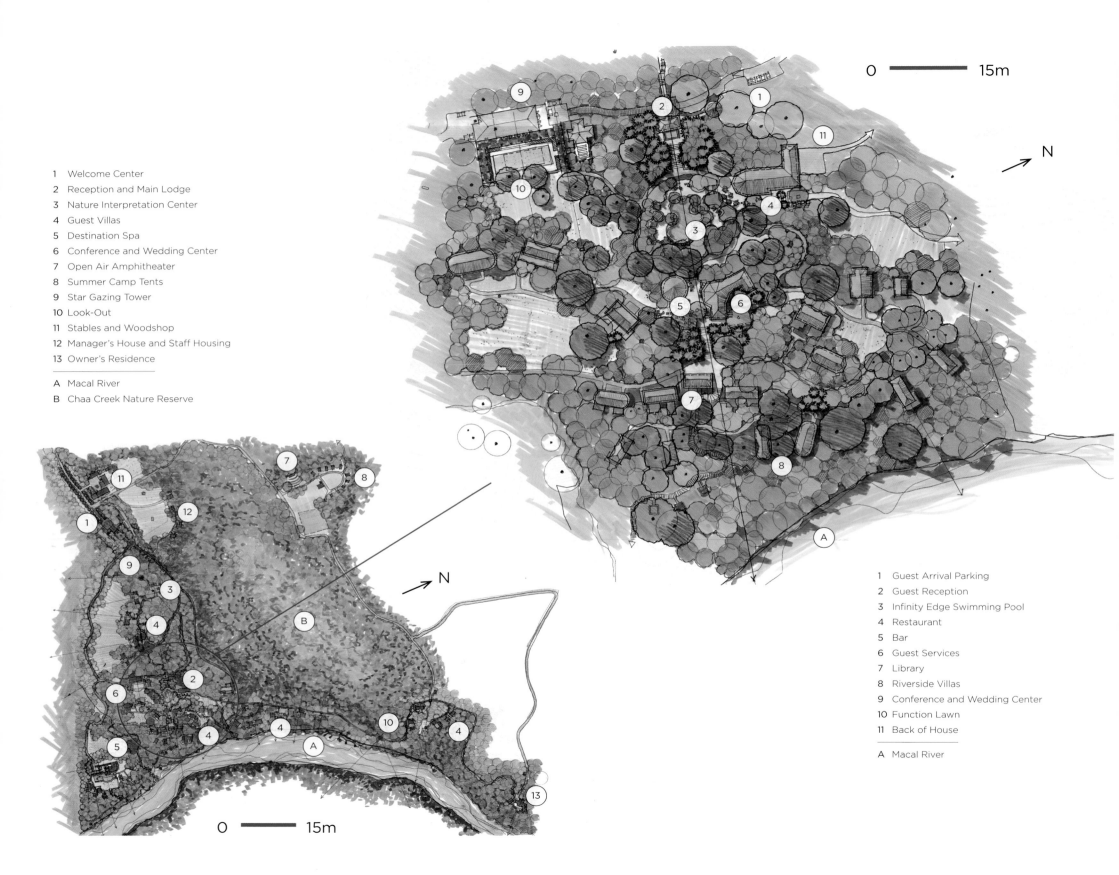

1 Welcome Center
2 Reception and Main Lodge
3 Nature Interpretation Center
4 Guest Villas
5 Destination Spa
6 Conference and Wedding Center
7 Open Air Amphitheater
8 Summer Camp Tents
9 Star Gazing Tower
10 Look-Out
11 Stables and Woodshop
12 Manager's House and Staff Housing
13 Owner's Residence

A Macal River
B Chaa Creek Nature Reserve

1 Guest Arrival Parking
2 Guest Reception
3 Infinity Edge Swimming Pool
4 Restaurant
5 Bar
6 Guest Services
7 Library
8 Riverside Villas
9 Conference and Wedding Center
10 Function Lawn
11 Back of House

A Macal River

O ———— 15m

N

evident in every development, detail, and daily operation at Chaa Creek, and ensures a continuing dialogue between the lodge's humble roots and its current status as ecolodge extraordinaire. Operating to the world's highest environmental standard, Chaa Creek is a model of energy efficiency, conservation, and sustainable practices, from the most basic, like what kinds of cleaning products and light bulbs are used (compact fluorescent) to more complex systems, like the Reduce, Reuse, and Recycle program. Additionally, in an effort to help support the local culture and preserve the habitat, Chaa Creek provides financial assistance to several local environmental, conservation, and youth organizations while simultaneously participating in several outreach programs, including the Black Howler Monkey Reintroduction Project, the Birds Without Borders project, which encompasses the study of neotropical migratory birds, and reforestation projects.

A true pioneer in the field of ecotourism, Chaa Creek continues to fine-tune its practices, and is always searching for new ways to perfect architectural and environmental techniques without comprising the land or its inhabitants. This is just one of many reasons to fall in love with Chaa Creek. The others are writ as large as the constellations that dot the South American night sky.

CUISINE: The Chaa Creek Restaurant utilizes fresh produce and fruit grown on-site at the lodge's 13 hectare (33 acre) Maya Farm organic garden. (Guests are encouraged to visit the garden to see the farming techniques mastered by the Mayan culture thousands of years ago.) Innovative dishes and drinks, like the sorrel flower iced tea, are enjoyed in the alfresco dining room.

ACTIVITIES: Among the seemingly countless tours provided by Chaa Creek are Mayan archaeology tours of Xunantunich, Cahal Pech, El Pilar, and Caracol; caving expeditions of Actun Tunichil Muknal, Chompiate Cave at Chechem Ha, Barton Creek Cave, and Cave Branch River; trekking tours of Vaca Plateau, Macal River Valley, and Mountain Pine Ridge.

DAINTREE ECOLODGE AND SPA
QUEENSLAND, AUSTRALIA

DATE COMPLETED
1995

OWNERS
Terry and Cathy Maloney

ARCHITECT
John Ewin-Smith (Australia)

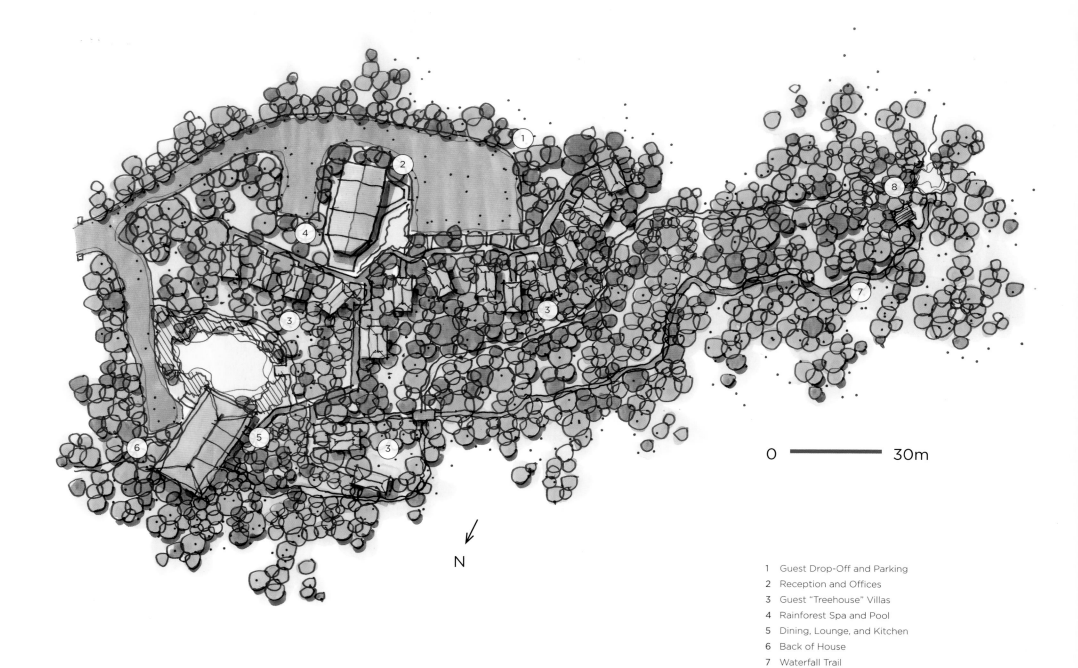

N

0 ——— 30m

1 Guest Drop-Off and Parking
2 Reception and Offices
3 Guest "Treehouse" Villas
4 Rainforest Spa and Pool
5 Dining, Lounge, and Kitchen
6 Back of House
7 Waterfall Trail
8 Waterfall and Massage Deck

Daintree Ecolodge and Spa invites guests to discover nature through ancient Aboriginal traditions and wellness techniques. Favoring the use of local plants and herbs for their medicinal and healing properties, the spa emphasizes native certified organic fruit, flowers, nuts, and seeds in their oil treatments. The spa uses pristine rainwater, sourced from the property's waterfall site, and superfine ochers in many of the spa's wellness products, too. The spa menu has been approved by the local Kuku Yalanji elders. The spa's goal, as with everything else at Daintree, is to integrate the wisdom of ancient culture, medicine, and healing into naturopathy modalities. Nothing at Daintree Ecolodge and Spa is complicated or over-the-top; rather, the experience is meant to be simple, harmonious, and honest.

Located at the tip of Cape Tribulation—the only place on earth where two World Heritage National Parks (Great Barrier Reef and Daintree) meet—in the world's oldest-living rain forest, Daintree Ecolodge literally soars above the rain forest canopy in fifteen treehouse-like villas. Lightweight materials, such as local timbers and fiber cement cladding, keep the architectural approach light and airy. The louvered windows reflect traditional Queenslander architecture. Walls and column roofs are painted green so the lodge's exterior seamlessly melds with its surroundings. Wooden interlocking walkways connect each villa, allowing guests to get up close to the tropical plants and trees and feel as though they are living within the rain forest itself. For this change of perspective alone, Daintree Ecolodge and Spa is worth the visit.

Of all the lodges in Australia, Daintree Ecolodge and Spa does the most to help benefit local Aboriginal peoples. It started the Karrba (Healing) Foundation, which supports the education, health, and well-being of Aboriginal people. Over thirty-six Aboriginal people have worked at the lodge, and many have moved on to become champions in their own fields. Twice a year, students from grade ten come to the lodge to learn about lodge operation, and the spa invites five to six Aboriginal kids for a two- to three-day educational program in wellness and health. The gallery also helps sell local handicrafts and paintings.

CUISINE: The Julaymba Restaurant & Gallery overlooks a peaceful water pond and serves innovative contemporary Australian cuisine with a native twist. Its menu has been created using the advice of local Aboriginal people and incorporates exotic fruits.

ACTIVITIES: Join the Aboriginal guide for an easy rain forest walk to the property's sacred natural waterfall and gain a glimpse into local Kuku Yalanji Aboriginal history, culture, traditions, and rain forest life. See exotic plants that predate the dinosaur era. Take part in an authentic Aboriginal art and cultural workshop. Enjoy total pampering at the spa. Take a boat ride on the beautiful Daintree River, home to estuarine crocodiles, more than two hundred species of fish, and seventy species of crustaceans. Finally, take a walk with a Kuku Yalanji guide or swim in the waters of nearby Mossman Gorge.

Previous spread: The lodge in situ, nestled in the world's oldest rain forest. This page, left: Lodge guests entering the Daintree Spa, which is unlike any other spa in the world. Products are made on-site from generations-old therapeutic recipes. Center: A guest luxuriating en-suite. Right: The villas are perched on stilts, tucked into the rain forest for a truly all-encompassing experience.

INDIGENOUS CONSTRUCTION TECHNIQUES

Indigenous construction techniques, which have been tried and tested over thousands of years, are being re-evaluated and marketed at a wider scale, and used at an increased rate in designing ecolodges. Indigenous techniques have many ecological and financial benefits: The production and use of traditional tools require low energy and have minimal impact on natural resources; tools are usually hand-powered and developed locally; and, finally, these techniques necessitate the use of local skills, labor, and knowledge, thereby contributing to the local economy. The ecolodges in this chapter have adapted and improved on old ideas with great effect, rather than simply copying ancient techniques. They have also bridged important gaps between modern market demands (electrical and plumbing) and beautiful forms from the past. The use of indigenous construction tools and methods has rendered the ecolodges to be more authentic within their cultural contexts, fitting closely into the fabric of local community life.

If you can, help others; if you cannot do that, at least do not harm them.
—Dalai Lama

ADRÈRE AMELLAL

SIWA OASIS, EGYPT

DATE COMPLETED
2000

OWNER
EQT International, Cairo

CONCEPT PLANNING AND VISIONARY
Dr. Mounir Nematallah (Egypt)

ARCHITECT
Ramez Azmi (Egypt)

MASTER KERSHEF BUILDER
Hamzah (Egypt)

Located near the Libyan border, an eight-hour drive from Egypt's vibrant capital city of Cairo, lies Siwa, an oasis so serene it rises like a fairy-tale mirage from the dry, hot western desert. Historically an oasis in practice as well, Siwa was used by caravan travelers during ancient times as a place to stop over and replenish resources. Lush with palm and olive groves, salt lakes, and over 230 natural freshwater springs, the area is known by the indigenous Berbers as Amazigh. Adrère Amellal could equally fall under their description.

Seeming to emerge from the sand itself, the lodge is comprised of seventeen buildings scattered at the base of the White Mountain, from which it gets its name. With enough room to accommodate eighty guests, the lodge features various lounge areas, dining spaces, and bars, all hidden from plain view but accessible should one have a penchant for wandering the lodge's cavelike interiors. The brainchild of Egyptian engineer Dr. Mounir Nematallah, Adrère Amellal is

an exemplary model of the use of indigenous construction techniques. Built of locally cut salt rock and clay—materials of the local *kershef* construction technique—and utilizing the expertise and labor of local Berber artisans, the lodge revives traditional construction techniques while simultaneously providing a livelihood for the local community. Built to minimize impact on both the fragile desert environment and to convey a "sense of place," there is no electricity; candlelight provides plenty of atmosphere. The diesel-powered water pump is used sparingly to preserve the lodge's most sacred feature: silence. Thus, no air-conditioners are used either. Instead, the lodge's thick exterior mud-plastered walls and wooden shutters are successfully enlisted to keep the desert heat at bay. Amenities are kept to a minimum, and all the furniture and crafts pay tribute to the surrounding natural palette and materials—palm trunk beds, salt rock and clay tables—and to local talented artisanship. Additionally, Adrère Amellal works closely with the local community, supporting projects geared toward making

Previous spread: The lodge, in situ, in the Siwa Oasis and with the Great Sand Sea in the foreground. Opposite page, clockwise from top right: For a truly memorable experience, guests can dine beneath the open desert sky; Local Siwa waiters serving cold beverages in the hot desert sun; Rather than using solar panels, the ecolodge is outfitted with tiny square windows framed with local palm logs, and walls made with a translucent alabaster-like rock salt that lets in daylight while keeping out heat and cold; The lodge blends effortlessly into the earth colors of the Oasis and Great Sand Sea (in the background); The oasis's giant salt lake. The area is populated with 300,000 palm trees, which are nourished by natural springs. This page, left: The kershef technique helps the ecolodge become a natural extension of the White Mountain.

Above: Each of the ecolodge's hand-built forty rooms is a unique experience. With no electricity, the rooms are lit with beeswax candles. Right: The Presidential Villa is the most luxurious spatial interior living experience at Adrère.

Siwa a center of sustainable development, including the Siwa Heritage Conservation Committee and the artisan-based Siwa Creation brand, which employs several local girls in the practice of weaving and selling baskets. The lodge's staff is largely local as are all the craftsmen, who literally built Adrère Amellal from the ground up.

CUISINE: Most of the mainly organic food is grown on the grounds or sourced locally. For example, dinner appetizers include beetroot leaves stuffed with spinach and succulent zucchini from the back garden with florets still attached as proof of just-picked freshness. For breakfast, while watching the sun rise over the Siwa Lake, guests are offered sweet olive jam with pita bread. Lunch is served by the pool. With more dinner locations than there are rooms on the property, dinner is served in a different exotic location every night. The secluded grotto studded with salt crystals and candles is not to be missed.

ACTIVITIES: Guests can purchase authentic artifacts at shops and markets in Siwa town, visit the tall dunes of the Great Sand Sea, or partake in excursions with local guides that include visiting fossil fields littered with shells, sharks' teeth, and corals from an ancient seafloor.

N

1 Guest Drop-Off
2 Main Lodge Building
3 Guest Rooms
4 Presidential Suite
5 Pool Clubhouse
6 Library and Spa
7 Siwa Crafts Shop
8 Stables
9 Organic Garden
10 Covered Car Parking
11 Back of House

A Siwa Lake
B White Mountain

0 ——————— 30m

KAPAWI ECOLODGE

AMAZONAS, ECUADOR

DATE COMPLETED
1996

OWNER
Achuar Nation

ARCHITECT
Cornelio Montesinos (Ecuador)

Kapawi Ecolodge was conceived in 1993 by Carlos Perez Perasso (owner of Canodros S.A., a tour company), who partnered with the FINAE (Federation of Achuar Indigenous People in Ecuador) as a means of providing economic support and jobs to the Achuars, the local indigenous community. The nineteen-room lodge is stunning in its overall architectural form—seventeen elliptical-shaped buildings line the edge of a lagoon off the Capahuari River like pebbles washed in to shore—and rigorously upholds the indigenous Achuar concept of nail-less construction. Wooden pegs and sturdy vines hold everything together. The lodge's two central buildings—used for dining and gathering—are connected by raised boardwalks that support the cottages.

All construction was done utilizing local Achuar techniques, and it took two years and over one hundred Achuar and several other people to build the lodge complex. The cottages themselves borrow from the traditional *naweamu jea* (stilt house) concept, and are built entirely from

wood and covered with a complex thatched roof made of palm leaves. Each cottage has a veranda that extends on stilts over the Capahuari lagoon. These stilts minimize the impact on the surrounding vegetation, and provide the perfect perch to watch the local wildlife: hoatzins, tree frogs, green parrots, and blue-and-yellow macaws, to name just a few. River dolphins navigate their way up and down the waters in search of catfish, giving guests a firsthand glimpse into the forest's rich biodiversity.

The transfer of Kapawi Ecolodge and Reserve to the Achuar Nation took place in January 2008. The Achuar now own Kapawi and have signed a contract with Complexo Ecoturismo de Kapawi S.A. (CEKSA) to market and operate the ecolodge. Seventy percent of the locals work for the lodge as waiters, chefs, guides, and management personnel. A first for the local community is that Achuar women have also started working at the lodge. Before the creation of Kapawi Ecolodge, most Achuars depended on cattle ranching as

Previous spread: The lodge in situ, in one of the world's most remote areas of the Ecuadorian Amazon. Opposite page, clockwise from top left: A local Achuar in traditional dress; A poison dart frog showing off its beautiful patterns; Each room is decorated with handmade furniture and riotously colored fabrics that evoke the lively spirit of the Achuar people; A local Achuar craftsman demonstrates an indigenous technique. This page, left: A guest uses the Lagoon Boardwalk to watch birds on the forest canopy. Above: No nails were used in the construction of Kapawi Ecolodge, and all materials were locally resourced.

Above: The Lagoon Boardwalk doubles as a romantic outdoor dining location. Right: The Kapawi reserve rain forest provides the perfect backdrop to the lodge.

their primary economic source. Today, however, 45 percent of their total income is derived from direct employment at the lodge, and 21 percent is from selling their artistic wares to tourists. Considered the largest community-based project ever developed in Ecuador, Kapawi Ecolodge is a dedicated alternative to the traditional model of construction and destruction that has long dominated the building practices in the Amazon rain forest.

As a culture, the Achuar believe in anthropomorphism, the importance of dreams, and the spirit world, something to which the Amazon rain forest is most conducive with its fervent, surreal lushness, prehistoric appearance, and cacophony of strange animal calls. The Achuar believe that when they die, their lungs become butterflies. Kapawi is an architectural manifestation of this intense belief system: the idea that dreams become reality and everything, everyone

is connected—not hammered together with nails, but harmoniously integrated so that the sum of each part creates a visionary whole. Kapawi definitely has the *Arutam*, meaning "spirit of place" in the Achuar language.

CUISINE: Meals are prepared by an excellent culinary staff, and include classic light cuisine, as well as Achuar dishes. The kitchen also does a wonderful job of accommodating guests with special dietary requests.

ACTIVITIES: There is never a shortage of things to do at Kapawi: bird-watching; self-guided forest hiking; night canoeing; macaw clay lick expeditions; night guided hikes; swimming and tubing; and kayaking and canoeing. A must is a visit to the Achuar community, which gives guests authentic insights into traditional Achuar living.

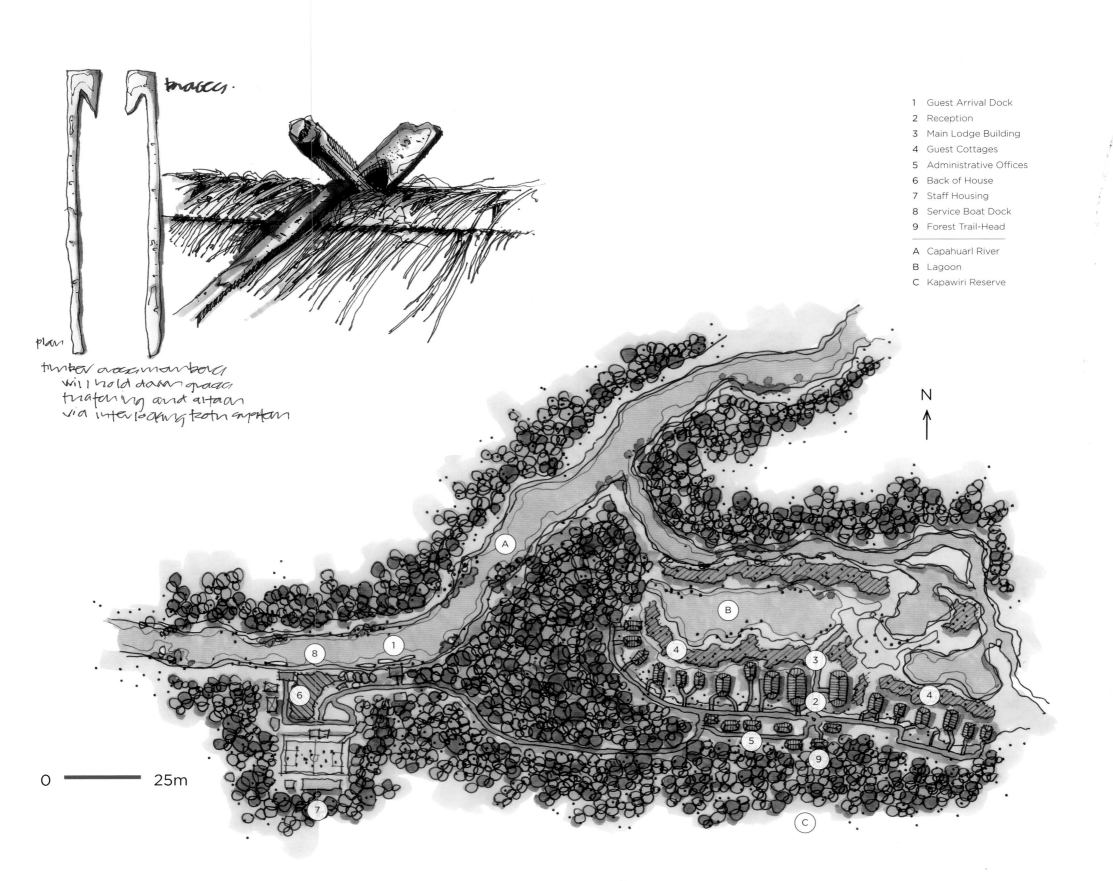

bracce.

plan

timber accommodation
will hold down grass
thatching and attach
via interlocking roth system

1   Guest Arrival Dock
2   Reception
3   Main Lodge Building
4   Guest Cottages
5   Administrative Offices
6   Back of House
7   Staff Housing
8   Service Boat Dock
9   Forest Trail-Head

A   Capahuarl River
B   Lagoon
C   Kapawiri Reserve

N

0 —— 25m

KAYA MAWA

LIKOMA ISLAND, MALAWI

DATE COMPLETED
2001

OWNERS
James Lightfoot, Nick Brown, and Ben Parker

DESIGNERS
Andrew Came and Will Sutton (England)

Built in one of the most isolated corners of Malawi—over 70 kilometers (43 miles) by water from the nearest town—Kaya Mawa is, quite literally, life on the far side of the earth. A model of indigenous construction techniques, not one power tool, drill, or cement mixer was used during building. All labor came from the island, skilled and unskilled. The youngest carpenter on the project was fifty and the oldest was sixty-seven. Timber was hand cut using pitsaws in the forest; planks were carried atop workers' heads to the building site, where they were hand planed and placed on-site. Every piece of furniture—from the chairs to the tables to the shelves—was also built on-site. A small fleet of island-born stonemasons placed every rock on the premises by hand, often scaling over homemade blue gum and bamboo scaffolding to get to each precision point. A tour de force of indigenous construction techniques, Kaya Mawa also excels in other areas of ecoconservationism—from its preservation programs to its use of solar power to, most important, its emphasis on creating a self-sufficient community.

The lodge consists of fifteen stone and thatch cottages, eight of which are hewn out of the granite headland. The Honeymoon Cottage with its four-poster bed, an en suite loo with a sunset view, and a private deck is located on an island and is only accessible by boat. From 1994 to 2003, Kaya Mawa was the only renewable energy lodge in all of Malawi: Forty-five solar panels and three windmills powered the whole place. Water was pumped from the lake with a panel-to-pump system that was controlled by a box that altered the voltage, depending on the sun's strength. Today, while each guest room still operates on solar power and the office runs on batteries and an inverter, the rest of the lodge runs off the island's main electricity grid. (The government installed mains electricity as part of a "rural growth project.") With mains power, the lodge is able to pump free water to the one thousand people that inhabit the three villages surrounding Kaya Mawa.

Previous spread: The lodge, in situ, on Likoma Island in Lake Malawi. Opposite: A private villa in a rock-island in the lake. This page, left: A guest walking to his island villa. Above: Guests are able to put on their snorkels and flippers on their private decks and jump straight into the clear waters of Lake Malawi.

Above, top: A local artisan creates an interior décor item for the ecolodge. Above, bottom: A quintessential African scene within walking distance of the ecolodge. Right: The Main Lodge building with restaurant, lounge, and bar has a plunge pool that overlooks the lake shore.

The lodge is locally staffed, providing further benefit to the immediate community. Island Child, a charity organization created by Kaya Mawa, gives friends and visitors the opportunity to sponsor local village children through primary and secondary school. Other outreach programs include the Kaya Mawa Rangers, a lodge-sponsored football team, and financial assistance to the village Malipenga dancers for island competitions. The generosity of spirit goes both ways at Kaya Mawa. When Will Sutton, one of the lodge's earliest owners, fell into a coma, a team of village islanders carried his stretcher, in relays, 4 kilometers (2.5 miles) to the airstrip. Their quick reaction saved his life. The Kaya Mawa staff are more like family—to each other, to guests, and to friends—than they are employees. Perhaps this is the secret to running an effective and truly forward-thinking ecolodge: Treat everyone with the same respect one bestows to the earth, and the respect will return in kind.

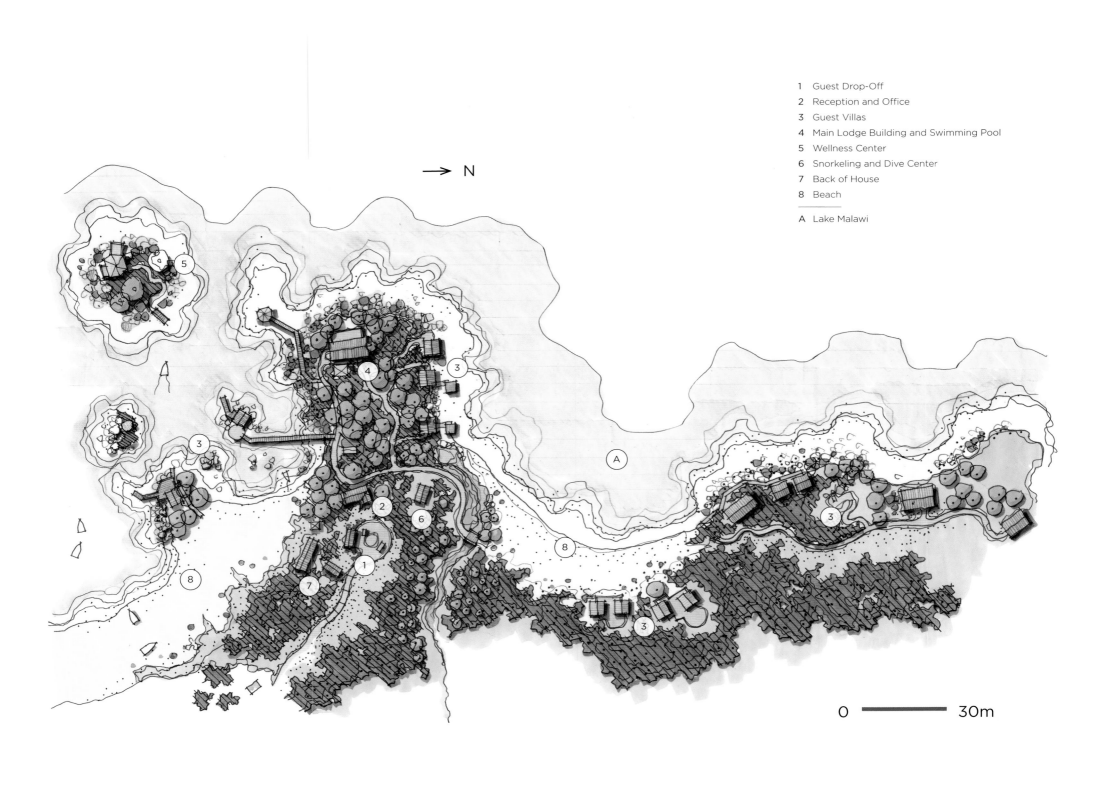

1 Guest Drop-Off
2 Reception and Office
3 Guest Villas
4 Main Lodge Building and Swimming Pool
5 Wellness Center
6 Snorkeling and Dive Center
7 Back of House
8 Beach

A Lake Malawi

→ N

0 ⎯⎯⎯⎯⎯ 30m

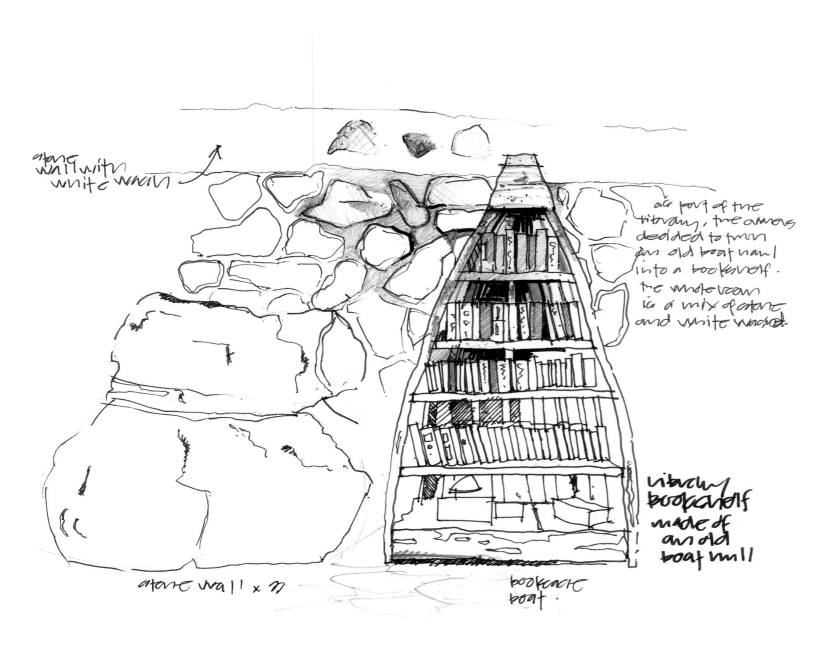

stone wall with white wash

as part of the library, the owners decided to turn an old boat hull into a bookshelf. the whole room is a mix of stone and white washed.

library bookshelf made of an old boat hull

stone wall x n

bookcase boat.

CUISINE: Local and international fusion food is served in the main dining area that overlooks the infinity pool. Or guests can dine at their individual villas while enjoying amazing views of the lake. Kaya Mawa also caters to people with various dietary needs. Most fruits and vegetables are purchased at the local market.

ACTIVITIES: The lodge has a full-fledged water sports and dive center. Guests can dive or snorkel in the crystal clear waters of Lake Malawi, which supports over one thousand species of tropical fish and has the highest species richness of any lake in the world. Masimbwe Island, which is located close to Kaya Mawa, contains several species of cichlid fish found nowhere else in the world. Other lake-based activities include sailing, canoeing, kayaking, paddle skis, waterskiing, and wakeboarding.

Opposite, left: A boardwalk leads guests over water to a covered gazebo perfectly designed for afternoon tea. Opposite, top right: Lake Malawi is directly accessible from some of the private villas. Opposite, bottom right: The rock face of the hill acts as the back wall to one of the private villas located on Lake Malawi.

BIODIVERSITY CONSERVATION

Biodiversity conservation is considered one of the prerequisites for an ecolodge to be called authentic. Not only are the three ecolodges presented in this chapter authentic, they are stewards of the land; their proprietors have excelled both in establishing and maintaining the quality of the local resources. The ecolodges have active and committed conservation programs and are also designed with sound environmental practices and are in accordance with land conservation infrastructures. Beyond this, however, these ecolodges recognize that their greatest asset—and, indeed, their best selling point—is the biological diversity of their surroundings, which happen to be among the most beautiful landscapes the world has to offer. Stewardship has never been so stunning.

We abuse land because we regard it as a commodity belonging to us. When we see land as a community to which we belong, we may begin to use it with love and respect.
—Aldo Leopold

CAMPI YA KANZI

CHYULU HILLS, KENYA

DATE COMPLETED
1998

OWNER
Six thousand Maasai members of the Kuku Group Ranch

DESIGNERS
Luca Belpietro and Antonella Bonomi (Italy)

Located within a wildlife corridor connecting Amboseli and Tsavo National Parks in southeastern Kenya, Campi ya Kanzi operates within the 117,000 hectare (280,000 acre) Kuku Group Ranch. This ranch stretches from Chyulu Hills to the base of Mt. Kilimanjaro with elevation ranging from about 915 to 2,135 meters (3,000 to 7,000 feet). The area's hills and ranchland were formed by recent volcanic activity—with some lava flows only two hundred years old—which contributes to the varied habitat of savannah grasslands, woodlands, and montane forest. The name Campi ya Kanzi means "camp of the hidden treasure" in Kiswahili, and with a name like that, there's little room for disappointment.

A superb example of an authentic ecolodge and deserving of every award it receives, the sixteen-bed Campi ya Kanzi is the result of a unique collaboration between the investors, the husband-and-wife team of Luca and Antonella, and the Kuku Group Ranch. The couple financed the construction of the camp, the local Maasai helped build it, and while Luca and

Previous spread: The lodge, in situ, at the foot of the Chyulu Hills, the Green Hills of Africa and overlooking Mawenzi and Kibo Peaks of Mt. Kilimanjaro. Opposite, left: Maasai-guided tours make for a memorable experience. Opposite, top right: Campi ya Kanzi is built in partnership with the Maasai community. Opposite, bottom, right: Guided 4 x 4 safari drives let guests safely explore the wilds of Kenya. This page, left: An aerial view of the lodge. Above, top: Local wildlife. Above, bottom: The ecolodge's architecture blends into the surrounding volcanic landscape.

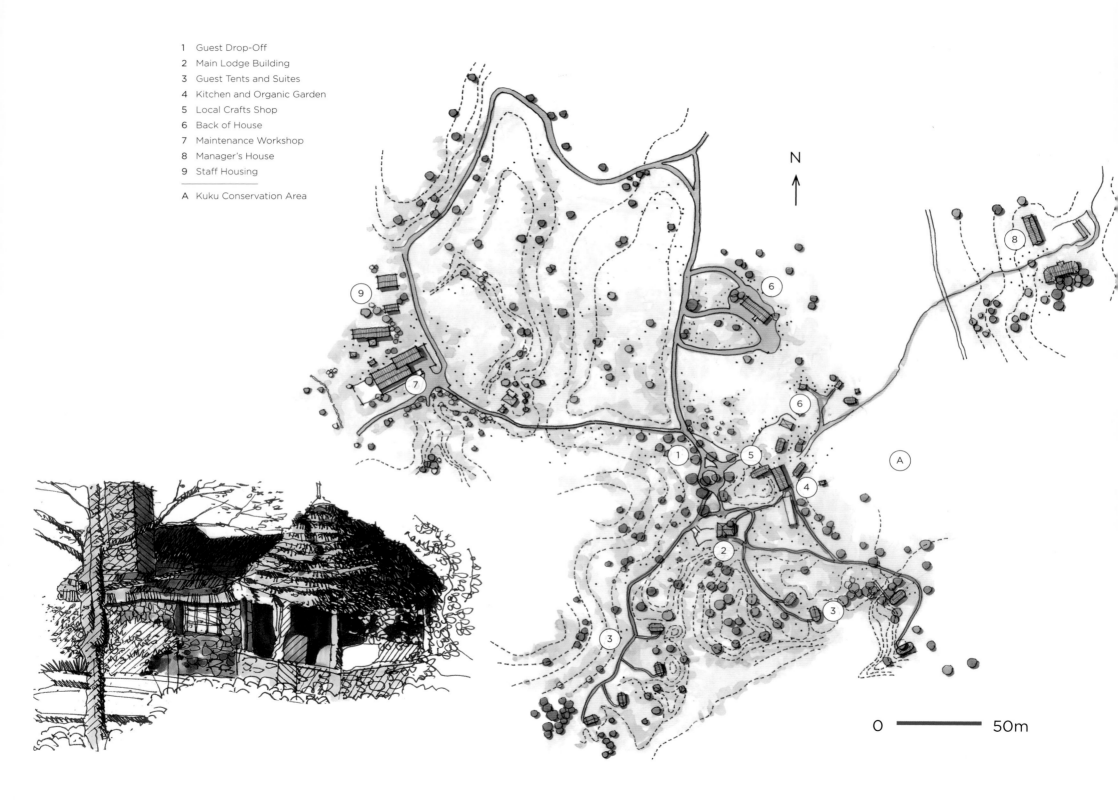

1 Guest Drop-Off
2 Main Lodge Building
3 Guest Tents and Suites
4 Kitchen and Organic Garden
5 Local Crafts Shop
6 Back of House
7 Maintenance Workshop
8 Manager's House
9 Staff Housing

A Kuku Conservation Area

N

0 ——————— 50m

Antonella have a twenty-year management contract of the 12 hectare (30 acre) camp, ownership resides with the Kuku Group Ranch members.

The major goals of the combined efforts of Campi ya Kanzi and the Maasai Wilderness Conservation Trust are to protect the area's wildlife, biodiversity, and cultural heritage. The Trust funds Maasai scouts, whose mandate it is to control and limit poaching, overgrazing, bush fires, and forest destruction, and to monitor and track lion populations.

A conservation fee of thirty dollars per guest per night is partly used to reimburse the Maasai who have lost their livestock to wild animals. The rest of the conservation fee and philanthropic donations from guests are used to assist with the employment of teachers and a local doctor.

Campi ya Kanzi is located in a transitional ecosystem with the woodland savannah giving way to grass and forest mosaic higher up. It blends into the landscape and features six thatched-roofed canvas tented cottages and two suites. Remarkably, not one tree

The African bush elephant (*Loxodonta africana*) is one of the species that benefits from Campi ya Kanzi's biodiversity conservation programs.

Above: The campfire is the perfect place for guests to connect and share stories of the days' adventures. Right: The Tembo ("elephant" in Kiswahili) House is the heart of the ecolodge. This clubhouse has a thatched roof and is constructed of local material, such as lava rocks and native timbers, collected in a national forest, where there is a sustainable plantation. Opposite, clockwise from top left: Interior of one of the six tented cottages; The lodge's lounge; Maasai Moran head beadwork; Typical reptilian neighbor; Ecolodge staff; Sunset.

was cut during construction of the camp. Environmentally friendly materials include volcanic stone and thatch grass from the site, wood from a sustainable forest in Loitokitok, and cedar for the lodge's bridge from a sustainable forest in neighboring Tanzania. Except for a generator, which is used four hours per day as a booster, everything at Campi ya Kanzi is solar generated, from the electricity to the hot water. No firewood is used in the kitchen, only charcoal made by UNEP (United Nations Environment Programme) utilizing coffee husks. All water is recycled through lava filters, supplying the vegetable garden and two water ponds where lion and buffalo come to drink.

As a genuine glimpse into the Maasai life and their savannah environment, Campi ya Kanzi is a truly unique opportunity to experience the real African wilderness. On clear days, the views to the highest mountain in Africa, Mt.

Kilimanjaro, are unforgettable. Campi ya Kanzi is one of only two lodges in Kenya that has been awarded the Gold Eco-rating certification by Ecotourism Kenya. And deservedly so.

CUISINE: The organic, on-site garden promotes healthful eating and meals are a social experience—all guests are seated at one long table. Once or twice a week, the lodge hosts a traditional Kenyan dinner—the perfect opportunity to sample local dishes, such as *githeri* and *irio* in their genuine setting.

ACTIVITIES: Whether attending the nightly dinner hosted by Mr. Belpietro, visiting a nearby Maasai village school, or participating in one of the many safaris, nature walks, or escorted wildlife walks, there is no end to the many ways guests can be inspired by all that is Kenyan.

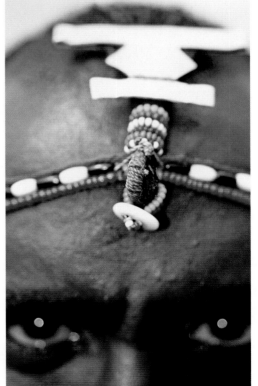

SUKAU RAINFOREST LODGE

SABAH, MALAYSIA

DATE COMPLETED
1995

OWNER
Albert Teo

ARCHITECT (JETTY RESTAURANT)
Johnny Liew (Malaysia)

A multi-award winner, Sukau Rainforest Lodge is an industry leader in Malaysia in terms of its hardcore commitment to ecotourism. Not only does the lodge help conserve the threatened rain forest and support local communities in a variety of ways, it also gives guests the opportunity to connect with the indigenous Orang Sungai culture on an authentic level. Located along the Kinabatangan River and at the edge of the lower Kinabatangan Wildlife Sanctuary, Sukau's surroundings are home to the endemic Borneo pygmy elephants, eight species of hornbills, twenty-seven species of bats, and ten species of primates (four of which are endemic), including the proboscis monkey and the silvered langur. The region has one of the highest concentrations of orangutans in Malaysia, over two hundred species of birds, and a remarkable number of butterflies and moths. With such varied wildlife in its own "backyard," it's no wonder that Sukau maintains an impressive facility for environmental education programs and has pioneered

several innovative conservation initiatives, including KWICORP (Kinabatangan Wildlife Corridor Regeneration Program), which is helping to reforest 25 hectares (64 acres); a bird rehabilitation project; an elephant research project; and weed clearing of the Kelenanap Ox-bow Lake.

With 70 percent of the staff coming from surrounding areas, Sukau is investing in helping the local communities. From repairing a local mosque to setting up comprehensive medical projects to employing local boatbuilders, the lodge believes in (and practices) giving back to the people. Driving the point home even further, since 2001 Sukau has systematically set aside one U.S. dollar for every international guest who stays; its sister company, Borneo Eco Tours, has contributed two U.S. dollars per guest who stays at Sukau; and four dollars is set aside as carbon-trading for every guest who takes a boat from Sandakan.

Set amid the tropical rain forest, the main part of the lodge is sited 30 meters (100 feet) away from the river bank and outside the riparian reserve to prevent storm water soil

Previous spread: The lodge, in situ, along the Kinabatangan River. Opposite: The entry boardwalk leads guests into the reception, lounge, and dining area to the ecolodge. This page: Over the years, the ecolodge has pioneered the use of solar hot water heaters, four stroke engines, and electric motors for river cruises and rainwater harvesting.

Above: Tucked away in the rain forest, the ecolodge offers several areas for private respite. Right: The Riverfront Restaurant is perfectly located to watch the activities in the river.

erosion. Sukau is built in traditional Malaysian "longhouse" style and on stilts to mitigate the annual river flooding. An open-plan concept is adopted for the lounge area and the Melapi Restaurant, allowing for unimpeded ventilation. Sukau seeks to maximize each guest's experience while minimizing his/her impact on the environment. To this end, the low-flow showers utilize freshwater from the river; rainwater is harvested, treated, sand filtered, and used in the kitchen; and recycling is a must. There is also use of solar hot water heaters, solar cells, and the recycling of cooking oil for lighting.

The lodge offers river cruises on locally handcrafted wooden boats using "silent" electric motors for close-up wildlife viewing. With four bird and wildlife viewing decks, a Rainforest Interpretation Center that details specifics about the area and its animals, and a 150 meter (1,500 foot) long Hornbill Boardwalk with two elephant "passes" to accommodate the regular migration of Borneo pygmy elephants through the back of the lodge, Sukau heralds a visionary approach to ecolodges and future biodiversity conservation work.

CUISINE: All guests are requested to don traditional Malaysian sarongs before they go for dinner. Robustly flavored local cuisine is the order of the day. The lodge also offers a romantic candlelight dinner at the Melapi Restaurant, which overlooks the river.

ACTIVITIES: Guests can take a two-and-a-half hour journey up the longest river in Sabah, the riverbanks of which are populated with every kind of wildlife imaginable, including proboscis monkeys and gibbons. Sukau is also a perfect jumping-off point to explore the *National Geographic*–featured Danum Conservation Area, home to the rare Sumatran rhinoceros, elephants, clouded leopards, orangutans, and 275 species of birds. Trek twenty minutes through the rain forest to the entrance of the Gomantong Caves to visit the indigenous bats, swiftlets, and crabs.

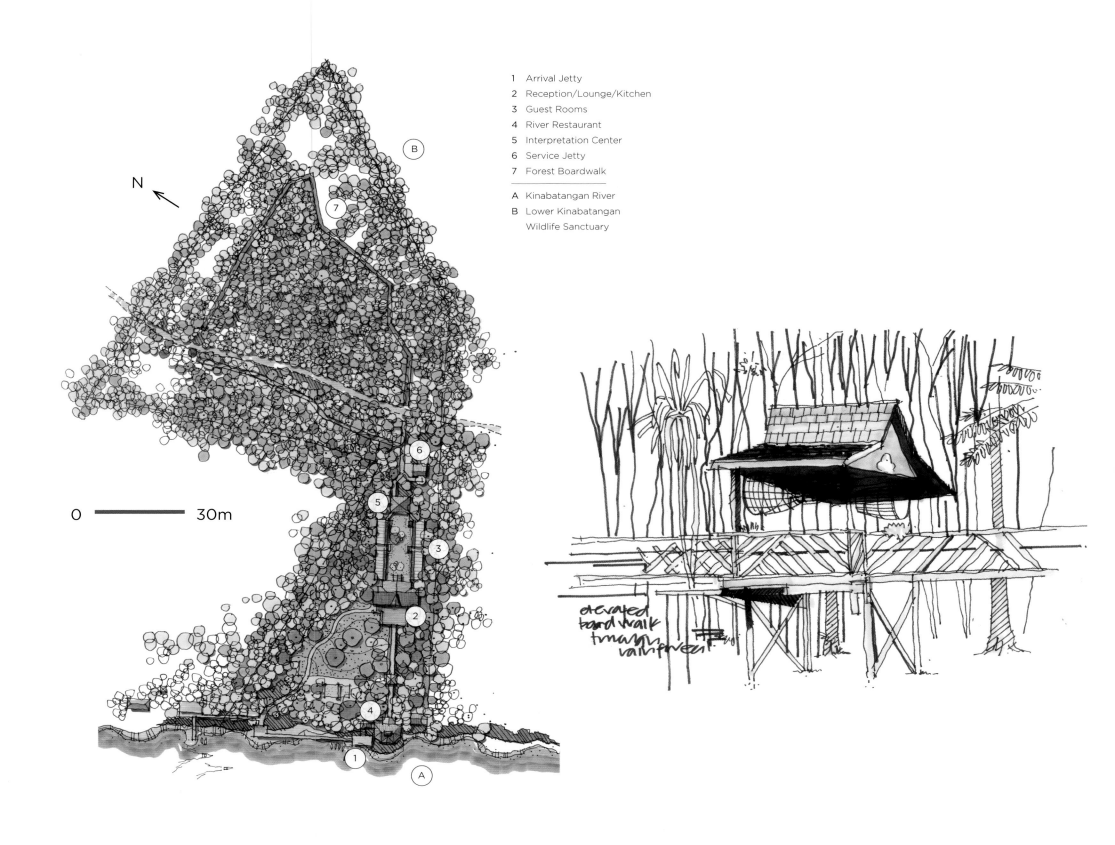

1 Arrival Jetty
2 Reception/Lounge/Kitchen
3 Guest Rooms
4 River Restaurant
5 Interpretation Center
6 Service Jetty
7 Forest Boardwalk

A Kinabatangan River
B Lower Kinabatangan
  Wildlife Sanctuary

N

0 ——— 30m

elevated
board walk
tmagn
vainforeat

DAMARALAND CAMP

DAMARALAND, NAMIBIA

DATE COMPLETED
1996

OWNER
Community of Torra Conservancy

ARCHITECTS AND INTERIOR DESIGNERS
Life Style Emporium (Pty) Ltd. (South Africa)

Damaraland takes its name from the Nama word *dama*, meaning "who walked here": The Damara people were known by the Nama people as those who left footprints around the shared water holes. Today, footprints are largely mixed with tracks from open-seater 4X4 vehicles; the area is one of Namibia's most popular for guided game drives and walks. While the dry Huab River Valley limits the population of big game, there are small herds of desert-adapted elephants and black rhino (reintroduced), along with the occasional appearance of more common plains game, like Hartmann's mountain zebra, giraffe, gemsbok, and springbok. Damaraland Camp is so perfectly secluded that visitors must be driven into the valley to reach it. Arrival signals a transformative experience, unlike few places in the world.

Located in the mountainous region of northwest Namibia, Damaraland Camp is considered an exemplary model for community–private sector partnership. The camp was funded by renowned South African lodge operator Wilderness Safaris, but is now fully owned by the local community. It was the development of Damaraland Camp that helped create the 352,000 hectare (870,000 acre) Torra Conservancy, the first wildlife-based community conservancy in Namibia.

Prior to Damaraland Camp's construction, the area was rife with poaching, both by local people and commercial meat and ivory poachers. There were no controls and the community had no sense of ownership. Today, this area has been transformed; the wildlife numbers are climbing and the animal populations have doubled. Black rhinos now form part of the largest free-ranging population in the wild outside fenced protected areas. The Damaraland Camp project has successfully linked conservation, poverty reduction, and empowerment. Before the conservancy's existence, most of its people were subsistence farmers who perceived wildlife as a threat to their livestock, but now they play a vital role in the sustainable management of natural resources in the area. Thus, the Torra Conservancy is considered one of the most

Previous spread: The lodge, in situ, deep in the Namibian wilderness. Opposite, top: Accommodation consists of ten adobe thatched units, with large viewing decks. Opposite, bottom, left: Local village woman. Opposite, bottom, right: Cyclical rainfall dictates the seasonal appearance and movement of the very rare desert-adaptive elephants. This page: Spacious living areas are open to the outdoor environment and encourage a spiritual communion with nature.

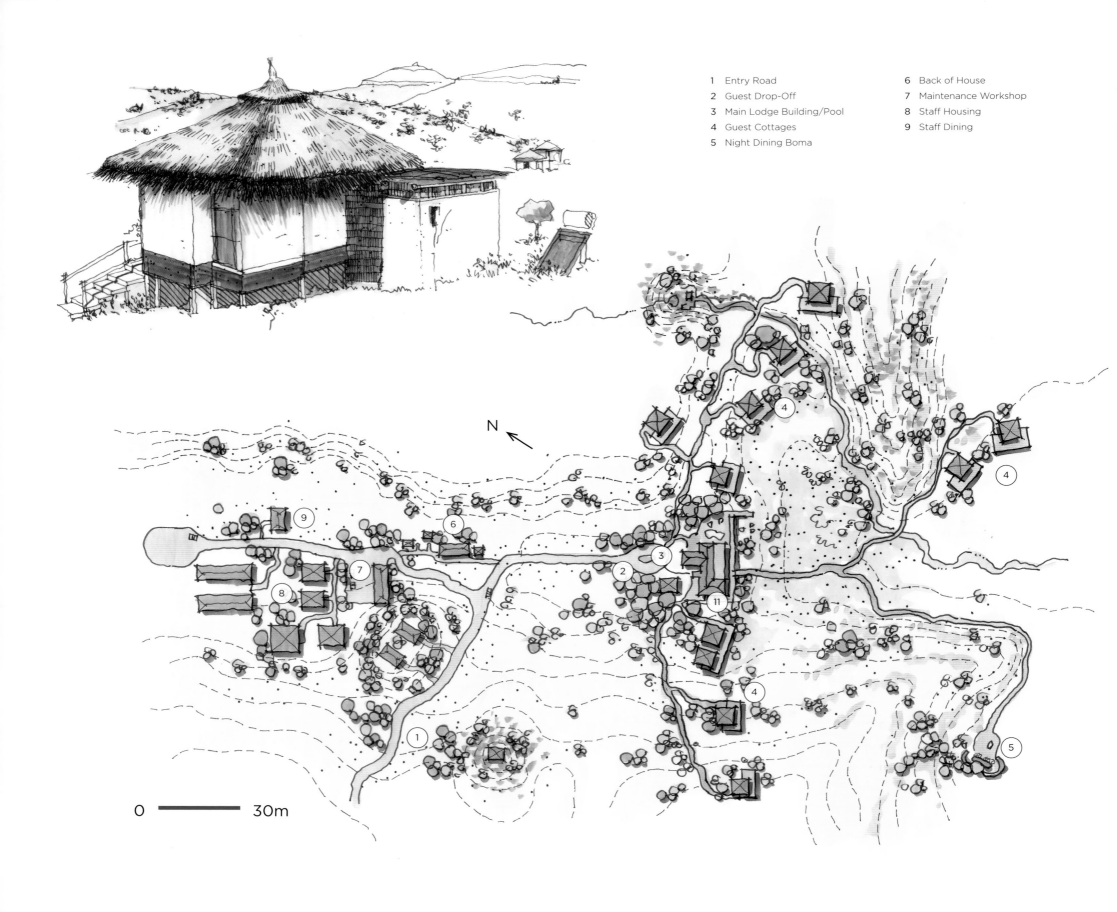

1 Entry Road
2 Guest Drop-Off
3 Main Lodge Building/Pool
4 Guest Cottages
5 Night Dining Boma
6 Back of House
7 Maintenance Workshop
8 Staff Housing
9 Staff Dining

N

0 ⎯⎯⎯ 30m

successful in all of Africa. Not only is it the first community conservancy able to sustain itself without donor funding, it also meets all its management costs and makes a profit, which is then reinvested into community projects for their benefit.

Graced with sweeping views across the stark plains, ancient valleys, and soaring peaks that form the Brandberg Mountains, Damaraland Camp combines the best of high-quality lodgelike living with ecofriendly standards. The camp features ten thatched cottages with en suite facilities that enhance the minimalist yet luxurious accommodations. Constructed from a mixture of clay-plastered "eco-sandbag" walls, reeds, and canvas, the lodge is on the cutting edge of safari eco-architecture, complete with solar-powered lighting using LED and compact fluorescent energy-saving bulbs, energy-efficient ceiling fans, solar water heaters, dual-flush toilets, low-water-use showerheads, and black water, which is treated in a bio-organic trickle plant.

CUISINE: The featured culinary experience is the outdoor *boma* dinner, which is served in a fenced area five minutes walking distance from the camp and under the starlit sky. Vegans and guests with dietary needs are well-catered for—a trademark hospitality trait of Wilderness Safaris.

ACTIVITIES: Activities largely revolve around game drives into the Huab River Valley or cultural tours to local villages. Trips can be arranged to the famous Twyfelfontein rock engravings or to track the endangered desert-adapted black rhinoceros. Stargazing presents dazzling possibilities with the crystal-clear African skies.

Left: The swimming pool, adjacent to the bar. Besides the bar area, there is an open campfire and an outdoor *boma*, an idyllic space for stargazing. Above: Local village girl.

CULINARY EXPERIENCES

Not only do each of the ecolodges in this chapter deliver exotic, mouthwatering local delicacies, they also offer memorable culinary experiences: ambient dining locations, organic, cruelty-free food sources, and authentic local cuisine. Conscientious healthy recipes are the order of the day (and night). A few of the world's ecolodges will not serve any fish due to the depletion of most of the fisheries of the world; others will only serve seafood that is not on the IUCN Red List. The ecolodges presented here combine the best of both worlds: superb locals with top-notch, fresh food, all served with a smile.

You forget that the fruits belong to all and that the land belongs to no one.
—Jean-Jacques Rousseau

LAPA RIOS ECOLODGE

OSA PENINSULA, COSTA RICA

DATE COMPLETED
1993

OWNERS
Karen and John Lewis

ECOTOURISM MASTER PLANNER AND
LANDSCAPE ARCHITECT
HM Design (United States)

ARCHITECTS
David Andersen (United States) and Alvaro Poveda
(Costa Rica)

Nestled between the Pacific and one of Central America's last remaining lowland rain forests, Lapa Rios is a true tropical paradise, graced with a dazzling array of biodiversity and dramatic scenery. A Minnesota couple, Karen and John Lewis, purchased the land in 1991 with the intention of proving a point: that a rain forest left standing is more profitable than one cut down. Originally conceived as a nature reserve with a bird-watching lodge, the Lewises quickly realized that there was a stronger demand for a full-service project. Committed to the idea that the land could be sustainable in both economic and ecologic terms, the Lewises constructed Lapa Rios around the rain forest (instead of the other way around). The lodge has placed into perpetuity 400 hectares (1,000 acres) of adjoining prime and secondary rain forest to create the Lapa Rios Reserve. It is one of only three properties in the whole of Costa Rica that has earned the highest possible ranking—five green leaves—under the Certification for Sustainable Tourism (CST).

Being located in one of Costa Rica's most biodiverse areas comes with a list of environmental responsibilities—namely protecting the area and its inhabitants—and the lodge works with the Nature Conservancy and CEDERENA to ensure that protective measures are in place. On any given day, guests can watch an impressive range of animals—troops of howler monkeys, long-nosed coatimundis, three-toed sloths, and over 320 species of birds, like scarlet macaws and toucans frolicking in their natural habitat—all of which is visible from one of the lodge's sixteen open-air bungalows. Built over 106 meters (350 feet) above the sea, the main lodge and guest bungalows stretch over three ridges and are connected by interlocking walking paths and steps.

During construction, not one native tree was cut down to yield the five-acre compound. Built entirely of native materials and featuring alfresco, solar-powered showers, the ecolodge has become a model of successful ecotourism as well as one of the Osa Peninsula's largest employers: 90 percent of its sixty

Previous spread: The Golfo Dulce beach. Opposite page, clockwise from top: Brisa Azul, the lodge's restaurant, which boasts a delicious menu of healthy dishes. Everything in the restaurant is geared toward sustainability, including the furniture. New chairs are made of bamboo; The ecolodge protects 400 hectares (1,000 acres) of primary and secondary rain forest; Guests can observe several species of rare hummingbirds from the outdoor dining deck; Detail, local artwork in the restaurant aids the culinary experience. This page: The lodge is carefully situated into the rain forest, and guest bungalows are connected via environmentally friendly paths—steps are made from abandoned railway ties, and handrails are plastic pvc pipes, for example.

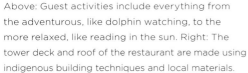

Above: Guest activities include everything from the adventurous, like dolphin watching, to the more relaxed, like reading in the sun. Right: The tower deck and roof of the restaurant are made using indigenous building techniques and local materials.

employees are from the local community. With five qualified guides that lead sustainability tours on everything from pigs, twigs, and garbage to learning how to take photographs of wildcats, the lodge's interpretation efforts are distinct.

CUISINE: It is the culinary experience, however, that makes Lapa Rios a true standout among the world's ecolodges. The Brisa Azul Restaurant, with views toward the Pacific Ocean, provides the perfect scenic backdrop for a sunset dinner. Staffed by eight local men and women, the restaurant has special *tico* nights, during which they serve only local foods. With an emphasis on creative vegetarian dishes, like black bean cakes, fresh heart of palm salad, coconut curry, burritos, grilled vegetable brochettes, and Turrialba cheese–stuffed sweet peppers, Lapa Rios was the first ecolodge in the world to have its own cookbook. Honeymooning couples can treat themselves to romantic lunches on the waterfall view deck in the rain forest and

savor what the Costa Ricans simply call the *pura vida*, the good life.

Brisa Azul is one of the first ecolodge restaurants in the world to have a special section for vegetarians. Every day, a local dish is featured on a table close to the viewing deck and guests get a sensorial interpretive experience as they taste the appetizer dish while reading about its ingredients and history. In the evenings, guests generally mingle at the bar, enjoying tropical drinks and sharing their stories of the day's hikes before moving onto the dining area for a four-course meal.

ACTIVITIES: With more than twelve hiking trails in the reserve (ranging from beginner level to advanced) and a virtual wonderland of wildlife outside every window—a haven for any animal-watching enthusiast—there is no end to the myriad ways guests can divvy up their days. Activities include surfing, ocean swimming, partaking in local village school tours, and enjoying on-site massages.

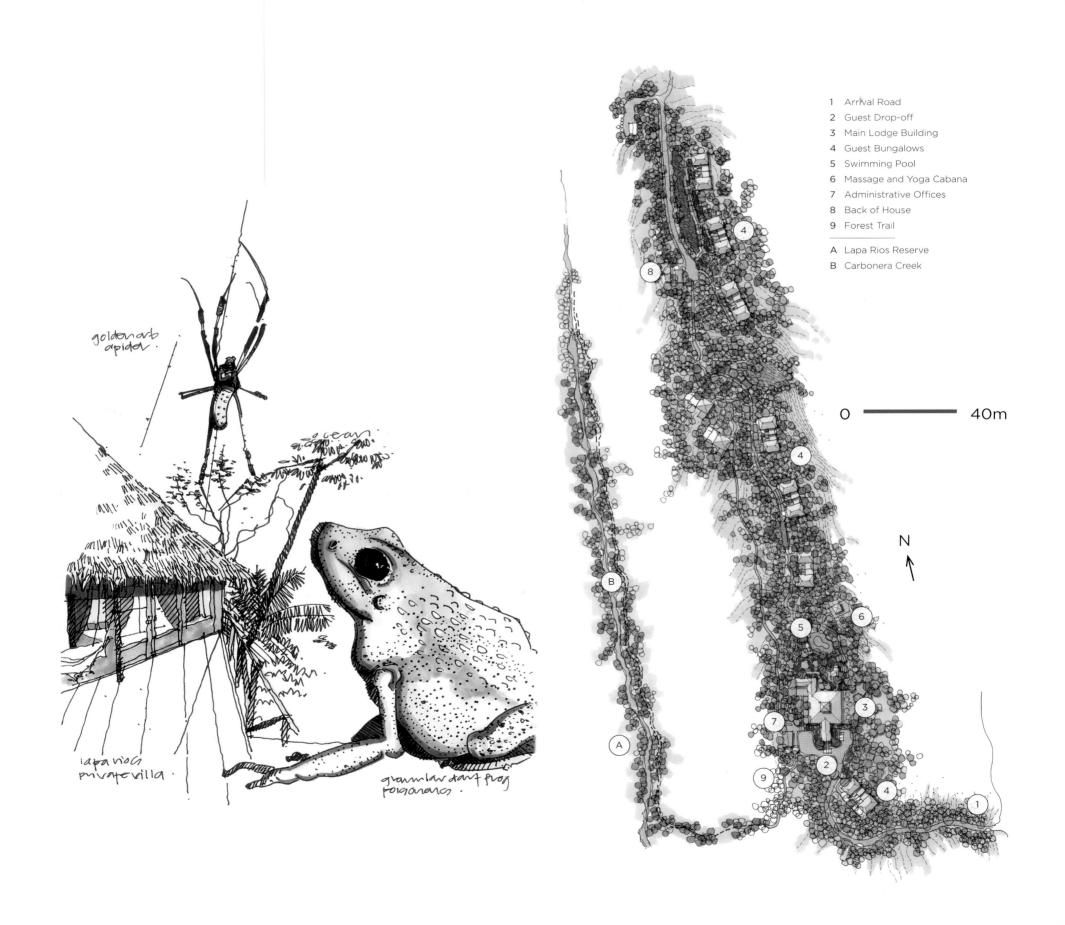

golden orb
spider.

ocean

lapa rios
private villa.

granular dart frog
oophaga

1   Arrival Road
2   Guest Drop-off
3   Main Lodge Building
4   Guest Bungalows
5   Swimming Pool
6   Massage and Yoga Cabana
7   Administrative Offices
8   Back of House
9   Forest Trail

A   Lapa Rios Reserve
B   Carbonera Creek

0   40m

N

SIX SENSES HIDEAWAY NINH VAN BAY

KHANH HOA, VIETNAM

DATE COMPLETED
2006

MAJORITY OWNER
Madame Ha (Ton Nu Thi Ha)

ARCHITECT
Habita Architects (Thailand)

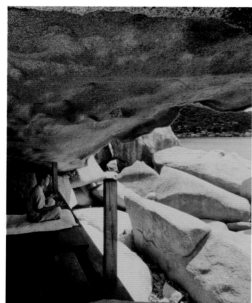

Six Senses Hideaway Ninh Van Bay is discreetly tucked away on a 1 kilometer (0.6 mile) cove of beach along the dramatic Ninh Van Bay and is accessible only by water. Sheltered within a cove of hardscrabble rock formations to the west and to the north, which provide protection from unpredictable weather, the lodge is comprised of a series of traditional Vietnamese villas designed to blend into the natural surroundings. Many of the lodge's structures, including that of the reception area and dining pavilion, were transported across the water, assembled on-site, and built with environmentally friendly materials like local bamboo, granite, and thatch. The boutique Hideaway effortlessly fuses ecosensibility with barefoot luxury, elevating a simple retreat into an unforgettable experience, one that is punctuated by a genuine commitment to the culture and lifestyle of the Vietnamese people. Each of the fifty-eight ample-sized villas comes with its own pool and breathtaking vistas of garden, treetop, or sea, depending on villa location. The Rock and

Water Villas are creatively integrated into the rocks and result in a harmonious relationship between building and landscape. And while the room amenities are nothing short of luxurious, it is the culinary experiences that establish this authentic ecolodge as a must-visit destination.

The majority owner, Madame Ha, is a descendant of the royal family and a master chef who operates one of the most traditional Vietnamese restaurants in the country. Her culinary influences are evident at the Hideaway. The dishes, prepared by head chef David Thai, are transcendent interpretations of East-meets-West cuisine. Traditional Vietnamese dishes are also offered together with drinks from the wine cave or healthy fresh juices and favorite libations from the bar. The lodge carries a full wine menu of over 250 selections. The added ingredient in all of the Six Senses' culinary creations, however, is the setting. With several different environments in which to dine—by the bay (where three dinners a week are accompanied by live local music); by the pool; by the

Previous spread: The lodge, in situ, on the dramatic Ninh Van Bay. Opposite page, clockwise from top left: Guest bungalows are sensitively placed into the impressive rock formation and overlook the South China Sea; A sampling of fresh food. The head chef, David Thai, was trained in France and specialized in Vietnamese food; Dramatic, water-themed entrance to the spa lobby; Local woman in Nha Trang carrying her wares to the market; Cavernous outcroppings provide inspired settings for personal respite. This page: White sand beaches and towering mountains make up the awe-inspiring landscape.

Above: A guest enjoys a swim in an infinity pool outside one of the water bungalows. Right: The architectural style reflects traditional Vietnamese design. Opposite: The Presidential Villa is gently situated within the rocks. Following page, left: Simple yet elegant entry staircase into one of the water bungalows. Right: Awe-inspiring architecture and lighting provide the perfect backdrop for the memorable culinary experiences at the restaurant overlooking the bay.

rocks; at private BBQs at the villa; on the jetty; in the wine cave; on a deserted beach in Nai Nho; and in a private cove in Hang Tien—no two meals are ever the same. The lodge also offers cooking classes and the one-of-a-kind *Six Senses Cookbook*, so guests can bring a taste of Vietnam home. An online culinary calendar offers guests an opportunity to book whenever the hotel has special culinary nights with visiting chefs or wineries.

CUISINE: In addition to the extensive menu, the chef and his team are sensitive to vegans, vegetarians, and people with other dietary considerations. With over thirty different vegetables and fruits from an organic garden, every meal is made from the freshest ingredients. Six Senses does not serve any marine species that are on the IUCN Red List of threatened and endangered species, like blue fin tuna or any "extreme cruelty" dishes, such as foie gras.

ACTIVITIES: Every manner of activity is available, from windsurfing and scuba diving to wine tasting and stargazing. With over eight tours, which run the gamut from Waterfall Trip Safari to Romantic Sunset Cruise, there's more than enough to fill one day . . . or one week. Guests can help local communities by traveling across the bay to ride "cyclos" to local markets and handicraft shops, see locals making rice noodles and rice paper, visit the white Buddha, observe Champa Culture Architecture (Ponagar Temple), or eat at a local restaurant overlooking the Cai River.

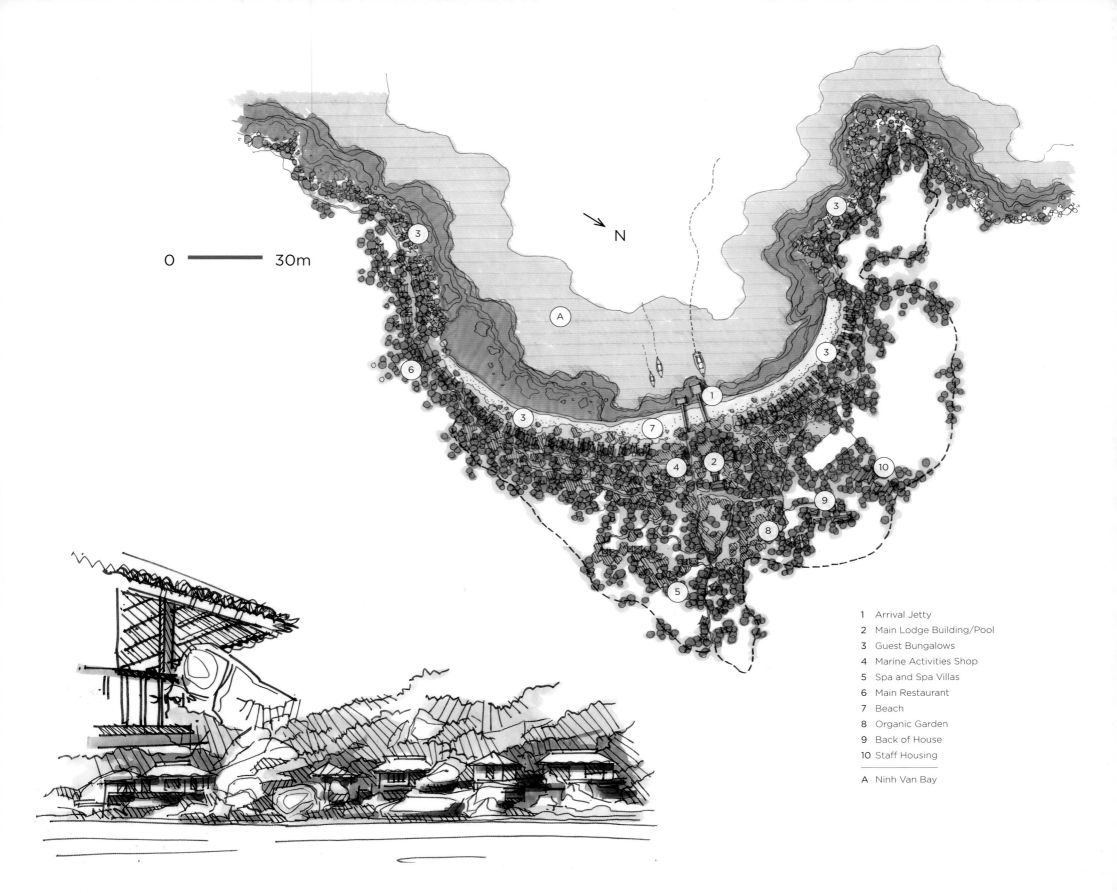

N

0 ⸻ 30m

1 Arrival Jetty
2 Main Lodge Building/Pool
3 Guest Bungalows
4 Marine Activities Shop
5 Spa and Spa Villas
6 Main Restaurant
7 Beach
8 Organic Garden
9 Back of House
10 Staff Housing

A Ninh Van Bay

TOURINDIA KETTUVALLAM HOUSEBOATS

KERALA, INDIA

DATE COMPLETED
1991

FIRST CRUISE DATE
1991

OWNER
tourindia

INVENTOR
Babu Varghese

Previous spread: The lodge, in situ, in the backwaters of Kerala. Opposite: A guest room is a traditional kettuvallam, measuring up to 80 feet in length. This page: The wood commonly used to make the boats is *Anhili*. Large planks are tied together using hand-made coir ropes and beaten coconut fibers.

Kerala, better known by locals as God's Own Country, is an intricate series of backwater channels, lakes, and lagoons nestled alongside the Arabian Sea, at the southwestern tip of India. Lush with flora and fauna, Kerala is a vivid ecosystem best discovered via a *kettuvallam* boat. In the local Malayalam language, *kettu* means "tying" and *vallam* means "country boat." While not a literal translation of kettuvallam, their significance comes into play when one considers the fact that kettuvallams are mainly constructed out of anjali wood and coir ropes. No nails are used. Boatbuilders, trained in ancient principles and building techniques, tie the wooden planks together, stuffing coconut fibers in between. The boat's framework is coated with a black resin extracted from boiled cashew kernels, which lasts for generations. These traditional boats, with their thatched roofs over wooden hulls, were originally used to ship rice, spices, and other goods. Their transformation from simple structures to floating luxury lodges—fully furnished in palatial

style—was the brainchild of tourindia's founder and owner, Babu Varghese.

Babu spent many years remodeling the old kettuvallams with the help of local master boatbuilders and tourists. He also made innovative ecodesign changes to accommodate modern lodging needs. Tourindia's houseboats range from one to three bedrooms with en suite bathrooms, a deck balcony, and a kitchen, with covered lounge and dining space at the roof level. Environmentally friendly materials like bamboo and coconut are supplemented with ecotechnology: use of dual-flush biotoilets that work on an enzyme technology imported from New Zealand, low-flow showerheads, aerated water taps, solar PV cells, compact fluorescent light fittings, and the use of four-stroke engines to power the boats.

CUISINE: There is no better way to experience the true nature of a people than through the local food, and in this regard, tourindia's kettuvallam houseboat kitchens epitomize the

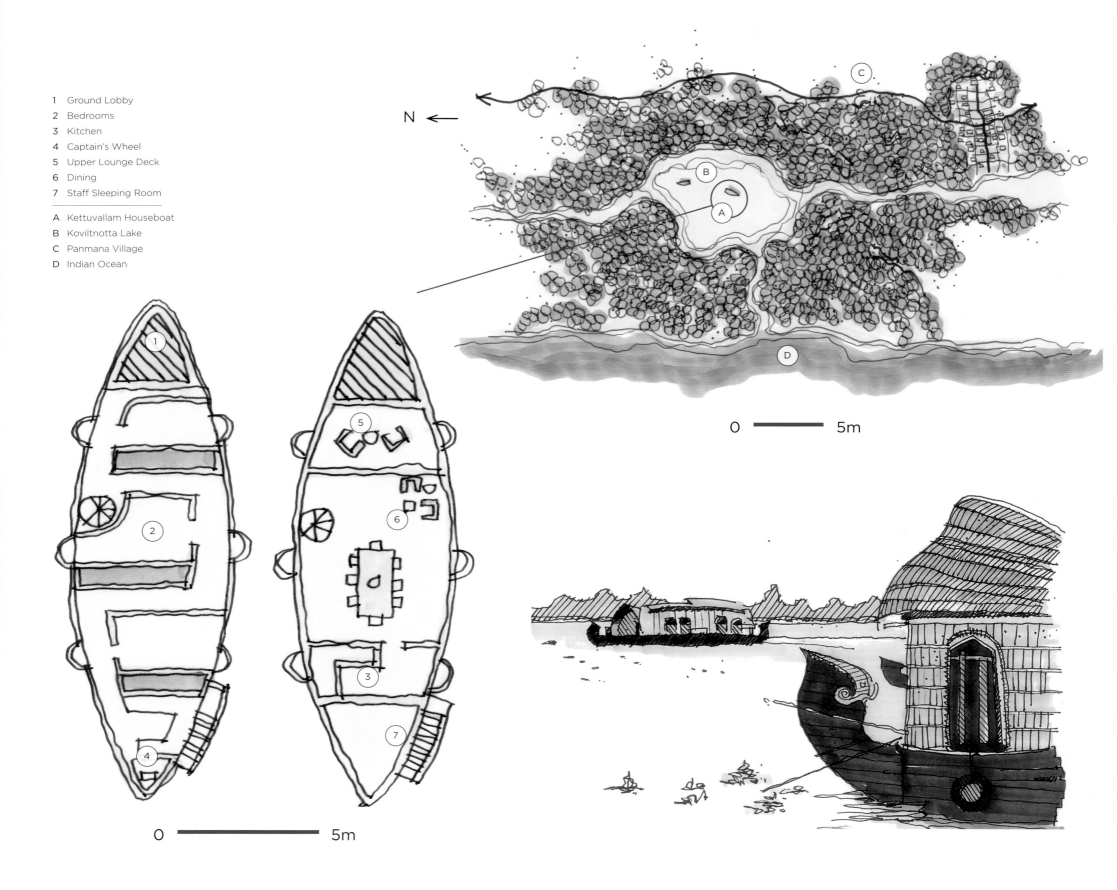

1 Ground Lobby
2 Bedrooms
3 Kitchen
4 Captain's Wheel
5 Upper Lounge Deck
6 Dining
7 Staff Sleeping Room

A Kettuvallam Houseboat
B Koviltnotta Lake
C Panmana Village
D Indian Ocean

N

0 ————— 5m

0 ————— 5m

south Indian way of life. The chefs use only fresh food and cook in the inimitable *kuttanadan* style. Since coconuts are abundant in this part of India, they are featured in nearly every dish. They are grated and treated as a garnish, mashed and used as a thickening agent for gravy, or their milk is extracted and used in a variety of ways, most perfect among them as a stand-alone beverage. The cuisine is a heady mix of different dishes, all adapted to Keralan taste. Spices factor into everything, with pepper, cardamom, cinnamon, chilies, ginger, and clover being those most generously used. An integral part of tourindia's kettuvallam houseboat culinary experience (as it is served most frequently at Keralan weddings and festivals) is *sadya*, a feast served on a banana leaf and eaten by hand with an array of vegetarian options, such as *puttu* (made from rice flour and cylindrical in shape), *kadala* (a traditional curry made with coconut, coriander, and red chilies), and *idli* (a savory cake made of fermented black lentils and rice). These flavorful options are followed by several different varieties of *payasams* (sweet desserts). All food is sourced locally and delivered to the kitchens via local transport: boat, bicycle, and rickshaw.

The tourindia kettuvallam team—from the owners to office staff to boatbuilders to the on-site chefs to the tour guides—are regional residents, making this a truly local operation, from top to bottom. A blend of home-style cooking with creative selections of savory spices and the freshest ingredients, all delivered amid environmentally friendly materials and technology, and with a breathtaking backdrop of serene waters elevate the Kerala kettuvallam from a historic cargo boat to an authentic ecolodge.

ACTIVITIES: Guests of the kettuvallam have the opportunity to experience the biodiverse 87 kilometer (55 mile) long Vembanad Lake, a Ramsar site; visit the unique Mannarasala Naga Temple; watch the Chinese fishing nets (introduced in the fifteenth century by Chinese fishermen) in action; pray at south Indian Hindu temples and churches; go shopping in local villages and markets; observe local women make coconut ropes; and, finally, visit a kettuvallam boatbuilding yard.

INNOVATIVE TECHNOLOGY

Innovative building technology can greatly affect everything in ecolodge construction—from the creative architectural details to the interpretive hardware (including shower pumps), to energy- and water-efficient equipment and the tools and methods of sustainable construction. For innovative building technology to be deemed authentically eco-friendly, it must be regionally available and easy to assembly on site. Replacement parts must be quickly and cheaply available and, most important, the technology must be understood by the people who are going to install and maintain it. While every ecolodge presented in this book met the basic criteria to be considered authentic, the three highlighted in this chapter have redefined the scope of what is innovative to awe-inspiring heights.

We shall require a substantially new manner of thinking if mankind is to survive.
—Albert Einstein

GULUDO BEACH LODGE
QUIRIMBAS NATIONAL PARK, MOZAMBIQUE

DATE COMPLETED
2005

OWNERS
Amy and Neil Carter-James

ARCHITECT
Kilburn Nightingale Architects (England)

deally situated between the Indian Ocean and the pristine African savannah woodlands, just north of the Quirimbas National Park, the Guludo Beach Lodge was created by husband-and-wife team Amy and Neil Carter-James, who wanted to make a difference in the local community. The entrepreneurial couple dreamed of creating an ecolodge that was as ethical in principle as it was innovative in technology. Guludo Beach Lodge far surpasses the couple's aspirations, and remains one of the world's most unique ecolodges, both in terms of its creative use of appropriate technology and its comprehensive community programs.

The lodge's award-winning design reflects the local style of architecture, and makes ample use of indigenous material like bamboo, coconut, and clay tiles made by local women—all to chic effect. The lodge's ten palm-thatched adobe bandas and canvas tents are seamlessly integrated within their natural surroundings; their presence gently frames the landscape, rather than distracts from it. Each banda and tent have a quirky alfresco outdoor bathroom. Positioned to the side of the private bathroom and up a small staircase, it has one the best views in the lodge—Guludo's breathtaking white sand beach and the Indian Ocean.

Guludo's use of technology is truly innovative. The shower fittings, made out of bamboo and located outdoors, are one of the most unique bathing technologies in the world. The dry composting toilet system saves water and so do the wash basins, which have no taps. Instead, water is provided in recyclable glass bottles. Additionally, Guludo utilizes several forward-thinking architectural and technological elements to minimize energy use at all levels. Thick mud walls, for example, are mixed with lime and calcium to help cool the lodge's interiors; the high roof maximizes airflow, negating the need for fans or air-conditioning. There is no electricity. Paraffin (soon to be solar-powered) lamps provide lighting as do guest-distributed flashlights and handheld torches; solar PV cells are used to charge batteries.

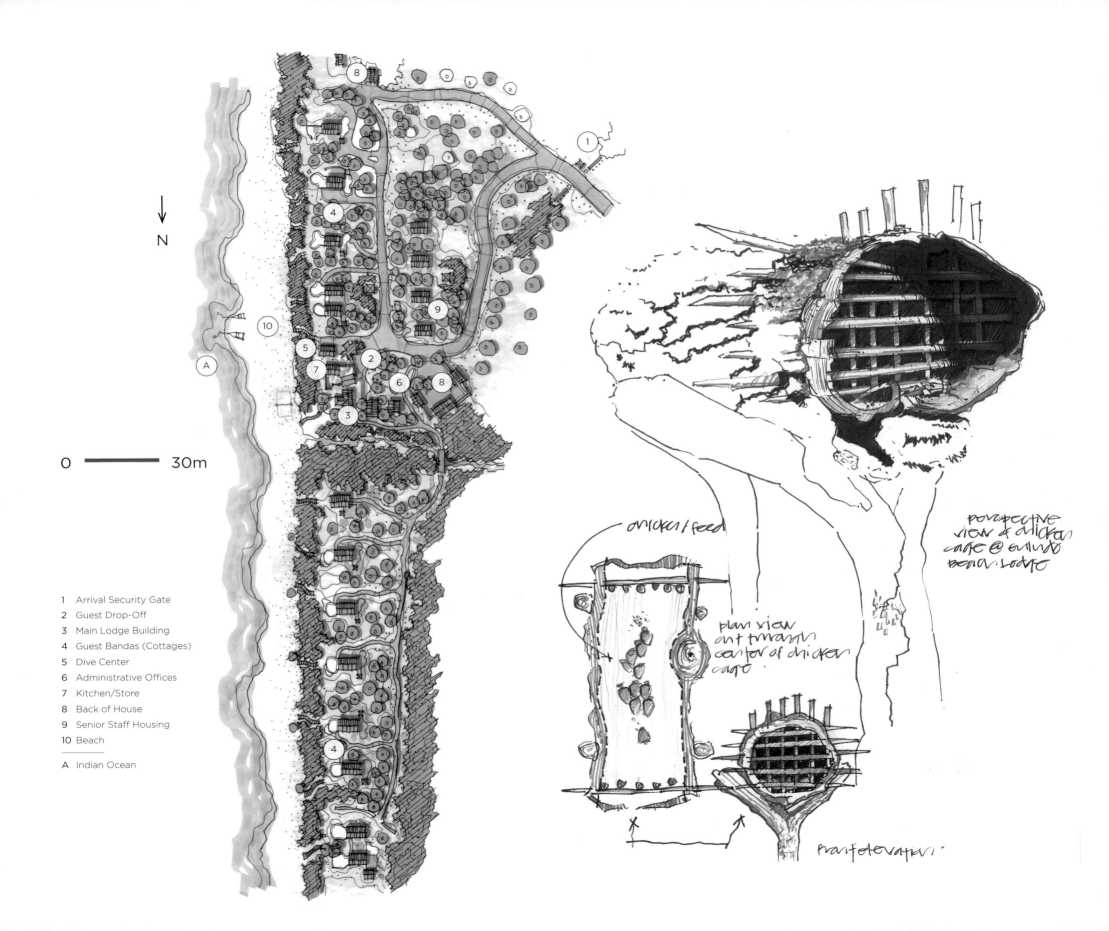

↓
N

0 ———— 30m

1 Arrival Security Gate
2 Guest Drop-Off
3 Main Lodge Building
4 Guest Bandas (Cottages)
5 Dive Center
6 Administrative Offices
7 Kitchen/Store
8 Back of House
9 Senior Staff Housing
10 Beach

A Indian Ocean

chicken/feed

plan view
cut through
center of chicken
cage

perspective
view of chicken
cage @ ensludo
beach lodge

front elevation

Constructed to uphold the strictest environmental principles, Guludo is a testament to the ethical rigors of inspired design and building technology standards. Where the lodge seeks to minimize its stress on the environment, it conversely maximizes benefits to the local area through the NEMA Foundation, which was established by the owners to work in the areas around the lodge to achieve their charitable goals. (The word for joy and happiness in Mozambique is *nema*.) Donating 5 percent of all accommodation revenue to NEMA, Guludo supports a variety of local-run community programs, all created to lift people out of poverty and simultaneously protect the environment. The Women's Craft Group, for example, encourages guests to learn from local women how to weave palm leaves or make traditional water pots. Guests can also purchase the artisans' wares, supporting the local community and its continued artistic heritage. The School Feeding Project ensures that every child at Guludo Primary School receives at least one nutritious meal a day. Guests can participate in this

project as well. In an area of the world where life expectancy is thirty-eight years, infant mortality hovers above 30 percent, and food shortages threaten the locals' health, NEMA is truly a lifeline to the people of Guludo. From its awe-inspiring design and cutting-edge appropriate technology to its sound ethical treatment of the local culture to its conservation programs, Guludo Beach Lodge promises a truly bespoke experience.

CUISINE: The majority of the food at Guludo is procured locally and guests can talk to the chef about the meals—and request their own specialty. Served European style but with a decidedly Mozambique twist, every meal at Guludo is a treat.

ACTIVITIES: With everything from scuba diving to savannah woodland walks to beach archery, there is no end to the adventures at Guludo. Unique to Guludo is the "beauty on the beach" group of local women, who give female guests traditional *muciro* facemasks and nourishing coconut hair treatments.

Left: Without a doubt, the most innovative use of local technology is in the shower, which is manually operated. Above, top: Detail of a joint at one of the bridges on the property. Above: Covered patio of one of the new guest bandas.

CONCORDIA ECO-TENTS

ST. JOHN, U.S. VIRGIN ISLANDS

DATE OPENED
1994

OWNER
Stanley Selengut

ARCHITECT
Glen Speer (United States)

ENGINEER
Paul Ferreras (United States)

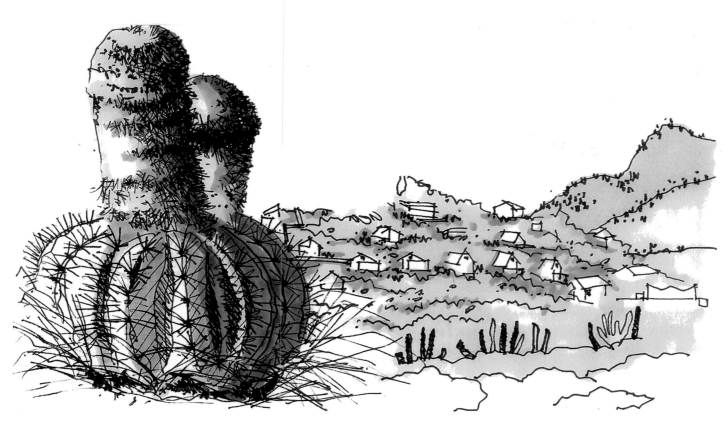

Located on 20 hectares (50 acres) of the Estate Concordia Preserve on the southeastern side of St. John—an area of the Caribbean that fits anyone's definition of paradise—Concordia Eco-Tents has been the most recent addition to owner Stanley Selengut's visionary collection of environmentally friendly ecotourism developments. As the sister to Maho Bay Camps, Concordia Eco-Tents elevates ecosensitivity to completely new levels. Designed to sit lightly on the earth—literally—all twenty-five of the solar-powered tents gently perch some 3 to 4.5 meters (10 to 15 feet) above the ground, allowing for both a Swiss Family Robinson tree house sensation and unencumbered views of the surrounding vista. Think white sand beaches buffered by gentle waves and a panoramic horizon of endless blue sky. Concordia Eco-Tents paints more than just a pretty picture, however; it is an environmentally sound ecolodge, satisfying all three of the compulsory criteria for ecolodges—conservation, communities, and interpretation—with a complementary host of other ingenious and earth-friendly traits.

Connected by raised solar-lit wooden walkways and a series of stairways, the tents themselves feature wood frames and translucent panels, large sections of which can be unzipped to reveal screens that welcome the Caribbean breezes inside. Each tent is equipped with the barest of necessities: running-water sink, propane stove, cooler, solar hot-water shower, and an odorless Clivus Multrum composting toilet that minimizes water use and impact on the environment. And, since the average rainfall is 75 centimeters (30 inches) a year, there is no potable water; drinking water is only accessible from central locations. High-efficiency photovoltaic solar panels provide energy for lights and appliances, and the electricity automatically shuts off when guests lock their doors.

Combining architectural ingenuity with ecological sustainability, Concordia Eco-Tents is easily one of the leading environmentally friendly technology ecolodges in the world. This unique combination can yield spectacularly innovative and artistic results. Some glass, for example, is collected,

Previous spread: The lodge, in situ, on St. John overlooking the Caribbean Sea. Opposite page, left: Crystalline waters set the tone for a memorable water-based experience. Right: All boardwalks, made from recycled plastic, are raised to protect natural drainage.

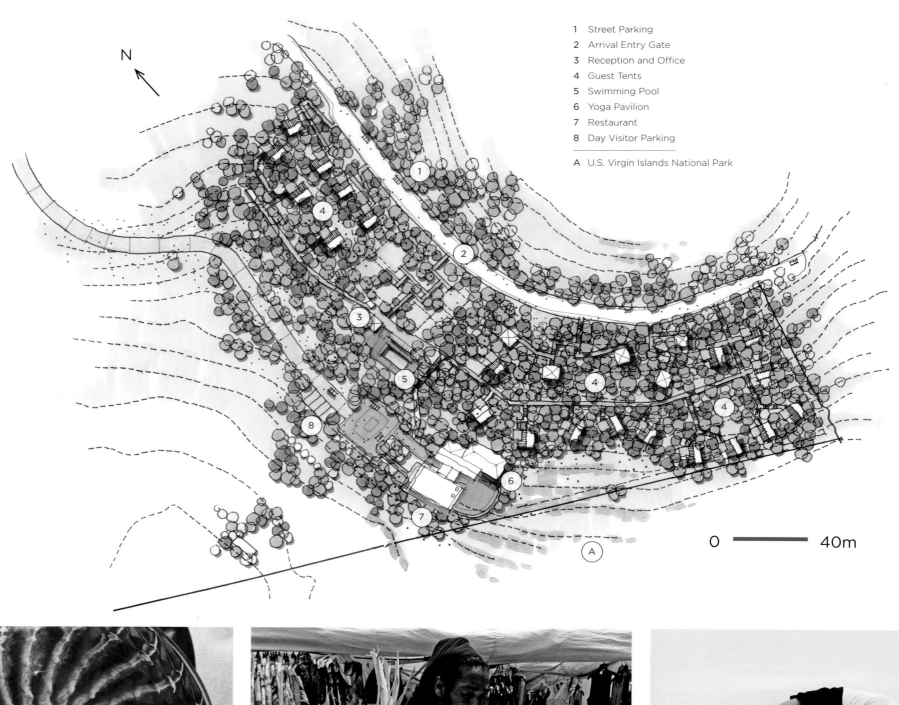

1 Street Parking
2 Arrival Entry Gate
3 Reception and Office
4 Guest Tents
5 Swimming Pool
6 Yoga Pavilion
7 Restaurant
8 Day Visitor Parking

A U.S. Virgin Islands National Park

N

0   40m

sorted, crushed, and sent to a special rebirthing station at the Art Center (located twenty minutes from the ecolodge), where it, along with melted aluminum cans, finds new life as art and jewelry pieces. Trash to Treasure is the first program of its kind in the world of ecolodges and speaks to owner Selengut's visionary concept—a concept that extends to the tents' showers themselves. As innovative as they are efficient, the showers utilize hand pumps to fill a tank on the roof and gravity feed solar-heated water to the showerhead. Guests physically pump the water supply, which gently reinforces the idea of water conservation. As if this weren't enough, Concordia Eco-Tents has also been at the forefront of design for differently abled guests, with several of the tents fitted with elevated walkways built for convenient access, wide doorways, easy-to-reach utilities, and spacious shower stalls.

One-hundred percent mindful in its design as well as its application, Concordia Eco-Tents gives back to its community, staffing local residents and hosting tours for visiting schoolchildren. All the goods are purchased locally, and the staff freely encourages visitors to check out the area's local restaurants. In fact, a night spent under one of Concordia Eco-tents' canopied roofs will make any visitor feel like a local. Maybe it's the sound of the ocean waves below or the gentle Caribbean breezes perfuming the night air; it feels like paradise.

CUISINE: The restaurant serves organic and vegan food and has a salad bar offering Josephine's Greens, locally grown in Coral Bay. There are also nightly vegetarian options, tropical smoothies, and several delicacies. The café, located on the lower level, offers alfresco dining with a sunset view.

ACTIVITIES: Besides the gift shop, there is a swimming pool, daily yoga classes in the new yoga pavilion, and an activities desk with information on ecoadventure excursions and biodiversity hikes in the surrounding area. During the high season, nightly glassblowing demonstrations draw guests and visitors to the Art Center, where local and visiting artists conduct a variety of mosaic, painting, silkscreen, and craft classes for all ages.

Opposite, bottom row, from left: Detail, handmade bowl (created from discarded wine bottles), which can be purchased from the gift shop at the Art Center; Guests at the Eco-Tents can learn about authentic local culture, such as the making of sugar cane juice in the streets of the capital; Guest at the Yoga Pavilion. This page: View of Ram Head and the Caribbean from guest tent.

MOSETLHA BUSH CAMP

MADIKWE GAME RESERVE, SOUTH AFRICA

DATE COMPLETED
1999

OWNERS
Chris and June Lucas (South Africa)

DESIGNER
John Bennet (South Africa)

Just three and half hours northwest from Johannesburg on the border with Botswana lies the Madikwe Game Reserve, South Africa's fourth-largest wildlife reserve. Managed by the North West Parks and Tourism Board and together with the private sector (lodge owners) and the local communities, Madikwe Reserve is operated as a joint venture to stimulate ecologically sustainable economic activity based on wildlife for the benefit of the people of the region. This community involvement thinking was something of a breakthrough in the early 1990s when Madikwe was formed, and has served as a template for other game reserves to work from. It has also ensured a healthily inflated local employment rate and zero poaching activity in Madikwe. Its broad spectrum of habitats in turn supports richly varied animal life. Of particular note is one of Africa's most endangered carnivores—the wild dog. For birders, Madikwe is a haven with the latest official list boasting an incredible 340 resident and migrant bird species. There is also great and intriguing diversity in the species of trees, grasses, and wildflowers.

Nestled at the very heart of the 75,000 hectare (185,000 acre) fenced reserve and named after the tree (*Pelthophorum africanum*) around which the lodge is built, Mosetlha Bush Camp is the only authentic bush camp in Madikwe offering a true wilderness experience. Unfenced, rustic, and intimate, Mosetlha accommodates only sixteen people in nine wooden cabins (laid around a central camp fire), ensuring the guests the best personal attention at the family-owned-and-run camp.

The camp takes innovative environmental lodge building and operations technology to a new level. The original concept for the wooden accommodation cabins was inspired by a camouflaged bird hide in a wooded area. Just like the hide, the cabins have partly open sides (used for ventilation and light) that can be shielded from the rain by canvas blinds. The foundations were hand dug, the cabins were raised about a meter (3 feet) off the ground, and internal spaces were modified to fit in beds, a writing table, and bush wardrobe.

Previous spread: The lodge, in situ, inside Madikwe Game Reserve and with the Southern Cross constellation in the South African night sky. Opposite, top: Game driving excursions make for unique experiences. Bottom row, from left: Meant to blend in with the surroundings, each cabin is simple in design; Lucky guests at Mosetlha can observe in a game drive one of the most endangered carnivores in Africa: the African Wild Dog; Each cabin is built from local materials. Timber is from a forestry area in Mpumalanga, and poles are made of eucalyptus and pine. This page: The ecolodge is harmoniously integrated into the Madikwe Game Reserve. Only the water towers show above the tree canopy. Prior to 1991, the Madikwe Game Reserve was used for commercial cattle grazing. With an annual rainfall of 300–650 mm, the vegetation is comprised of thorn bushveld, mixed bushveld, and clay thorn bushveld.

Above: Guest filling up the donkey boiler with cold water. Right: The lounge and library—a favorite gathering place.

The bathing technology at Mosetlha is extremely low impact. Guests fill a bucket of cold water from a water tank and then exchange it with hot water from either of the two traditional "donkey" boilers, which consist of a drum of water mounted above a fire. The cold water is poured to the bottom and the pressure causes the hot water to come out the top. Guests then add some cold water to the hot water and the warm water is carried to any of the three toilet and shower complexes discreetly positioned near the cabins. In the shower room, a pulley system allows the guest to lower and raise a steel bucket, which has an adjustable showerhead at the bottom. The eco-friendly toilets are black water-ventilated improved pit (VIP) latrines, and are comfortable and hygienic.

As a truly authentic bush camp experience, Mosetlha doesn't have electricity; it is lit at night by paraffin lamps. Solar panels are used to charge batteries and the staff housing utilizes solar water heaters. Cooking is done over an open fire and meals are 100 percent South African. It doesn't get much more

rustic than this. Mosetlha has a down-to-earth attitude that is both refreshing and welcoming. Their mission is to provide an exclusive and unique wilderness experience for their guests, with minimal ecological impact on the bushveld surroundings.

CUISINE: After dawn game drives, a sumptuous breakfast is served under the tree adjacent to the dining area. During game drives, the hoods of the 4X4 vehicles act as tables, and hot chai and scones are served while watching game—a memorable way to picnic on the wild side.

ACTIVITIES: The exceptionally trained field guides take guests twice a day in open 4X4s for safari drives in the early morning and evening. The daytime wilderness walk in the nearby hills is a must. And there is, of course, the roaring campfire around which to tell old safari stories and talk about interesting discoveries from the day's game drives.

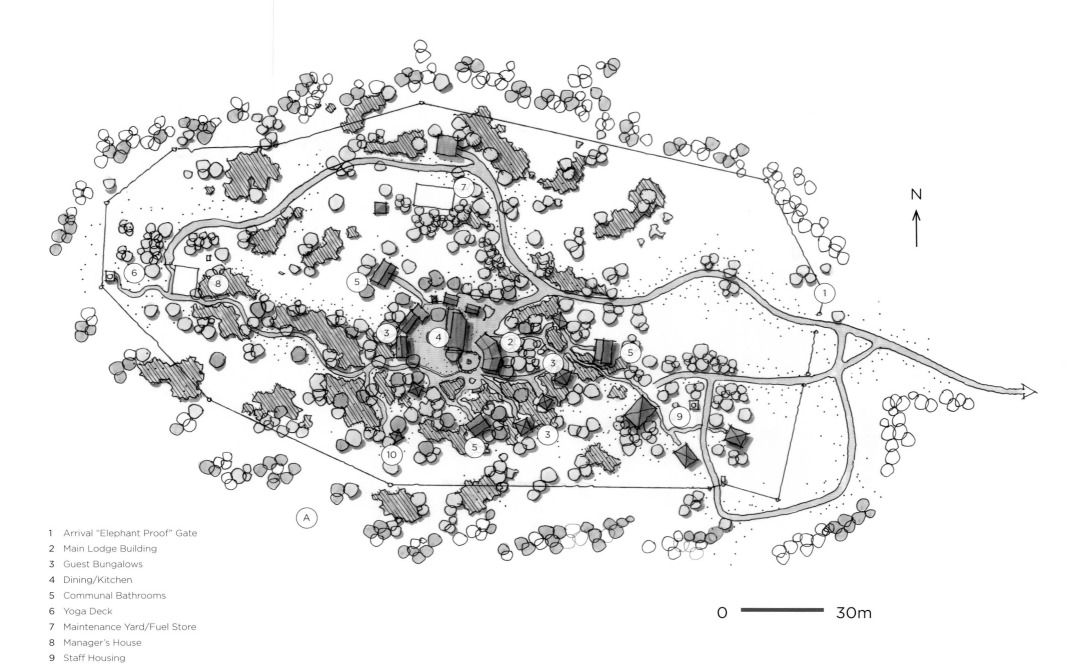

N

1 Arrival "Elephant Proof" Gate
2 Main Lodge Building
3 Guest Bungalows
4 Dining/Kitchen
5 Communal Bathrooms
6 Yoga Deck
7 Maintenance Yard/Fuel Store
8 Manager's House
9 Staff Housing
10 Security House

A Madikwe Game Reserve

0 ▬▬▬▬ 30m

ART AS ARCHITECTURE

This chapter celebrates those authentic ecolodges that cross the fine line between art and architecture. Inspiring in form and often integrating the surrounding environment in a seamless fashion, these ecolodges transform art into architecture and vice versa. The result? Truly transformative environs that work in tandem with nature. The ecolodges are playful yet sculptural in form and possess an organic quality that makes them artistically genuine.

There are three forms of visual art: Painting is art to look at, sculpture is art you can walk around, and architecture is art you can walk through.
—Dan Rice

LAS TORRES ECOCAMP

PATAGONIA, CHILE

DATE COMPLETED
2000

OWNER
Cascada Expediciones

ARCHITECT
Marcelo Rodriguez (Chile)

ARTIST
Angelino Soto (Chile)

The native people of Patagonia, Chile, were, by nature, nomadic, and they constantly crisscrossed the coast for food and shelter. As such, their homes were built on spec, utilizing organic materials found on-site. The Kawesqar people constructed their huts into a geodesic shape, bending branches to create the basic structure. Guanaco and sea lion skins were then used to cover the structure.

Located in Torres del Paine National Park, each guest space in the Las Torres EcoCamp is a modern-day rendition of this traditional hut, simultaneously resembling an igloo and a dome. The geodesic shapes of both the igloo and the dome are not only artistically dazzling, they also act as a shield against the powerful Patagonia winds. Both forms have a solid structure of galvanized iron covered with canvas coating and filled with synthetic insulation. The rounded surface also helps to disperse the frigid temperatures, allowing less exchange of temperature with the warm interiors. The camp itself is outfitted with twenty-one accommodation igloos, all of which

have vitrified wooden floors and ample sleeping space. The camp also has three Giant Domes: the Dining Room Domes and the Living and Resting Room Dome, which provide an intimate environment for visits among friends or simply moments for personal relaxation. Environmental systems at the camp consist of wet composting toilets that work with water, passive heating and lighting, a hydroturbine used for energy generation, solar PV cells for landscape lights, and small fans in toilet chutes. All waste is sorted, recycled, or reused.

Angelino Soto, an art teacher in a school in the nearest large town, Puerto Natales, was commissioned by the owners to paint images onto the canvases of the igloos and domes that would best reflect the historical and natural context of the national park. Angelino has painted masterpieces and each igloo and dome has a theme. Several have Native American peoples painted on them while others are nature based, featuring images of foxes, cougars, birds, and trees. By

Previous spread: The lodge, in situ, in the heart of Patagonia's Torres del Paine National Park. Opposite, clockwise from top: Each dome is hand-painted with artwork inspired by the native lifestyle and habitat; Futuristic in form, the domes utilize surprisingly simple technology in function; Local wildlife; View from inside the Lounge Tent, one of the geometric wonders. This page: Spectacular vista view of the Torres del Paine.

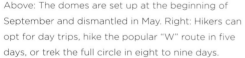
Above: The domes are set up at the beginning of September and dismantled in May. Right: Hikers can opt for day trips, hike the popular "W" route in five days, or trek the full circle in eight to nine days.

covering the whole exterior of each dome with an exquisite oil mural, guests feel that they are staying in a painting, rather than in a building. It is indeed, art as architecture.

Surrounded by topography as varied as smoky volcanoes, barren flatlands, and expansive ice fields, Las Torres EcoCamp gives guests ample opportunity to take full advantage of life's greatest amenity: Mother Nature. With private overnight departure trips to any number of local hotspots—ancient fjords, forests, or lakes—Las Torres EcoCamp encourages good-natured fun among guests, all in the name of enlivening the nomadic spirit.

CUISINE: All meals are served in the dining room domes and the camp also helps prepare delicious day lunches for those who would be trekking full days. Guests with alternate eating preferences are well catered for.

ACTIVITIES: The national park has unlimited beauty and adventure to offer, with glaciers, lakes, mountains, wildflowers, birds, trekking, and horseback riding to choose from. On an extended five-day Torres del Paine Active Tour, guests can see everything from Punta Arenas to Los Cuernos trail to Pehoe Lake to the lookout point of Laguna Azul.

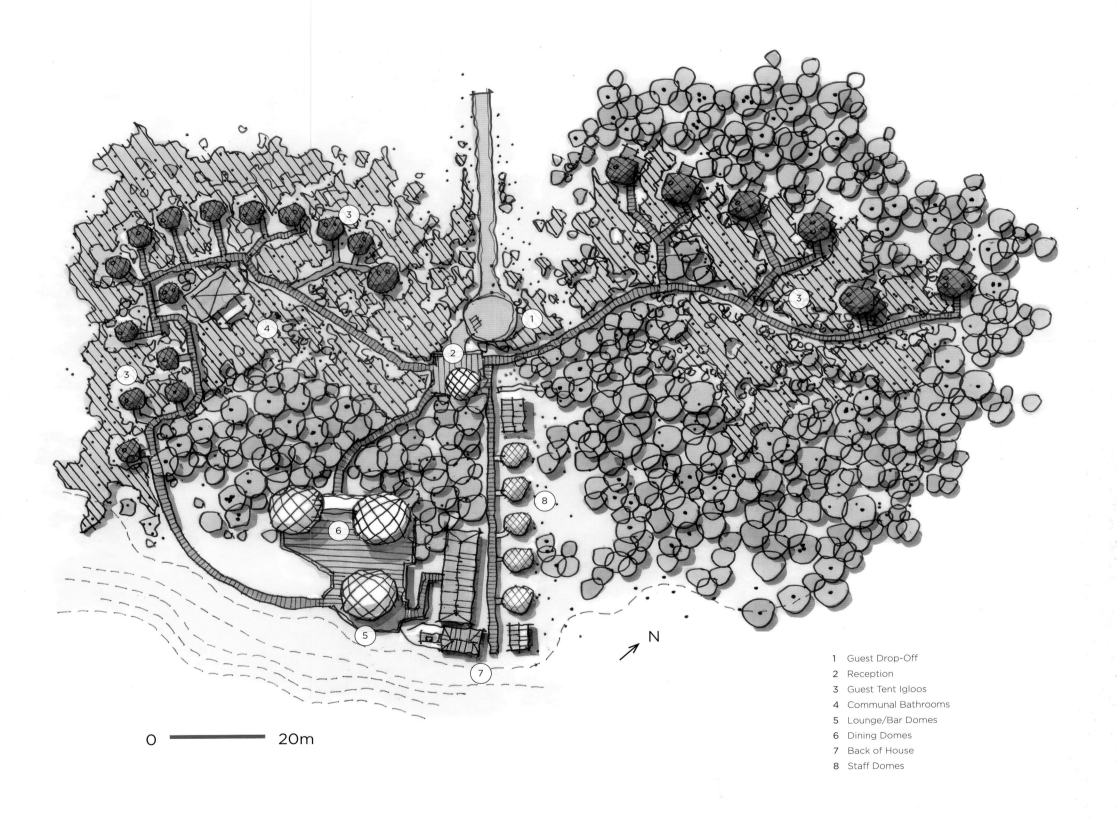

N

0 ———— 20m

1 Guest Drop-Off
2 Reception
3 Guest Tent Igloos
4 Communal Bathrooms
5 Lounge/Bar Domes
6 Dining Domes
7 Back of House
8 Staff Domes

ECOLODGE RENDEZ-VOUS

SABA ISLAND, CARIBBEAN SEA

DATE COMPLETED
2002

OWNER
Van't Hof Family

DESIGNER AND ARTIST
Heleen Cornet

1 Arrival Pathway
2 Reception/Restaurant
3 Guest Cottages
4 Sweat Lodge
5 Swimming Pool
6 Terraced Garden
7 Meditation Garden
8 Organic Garden
9 Back of House

N

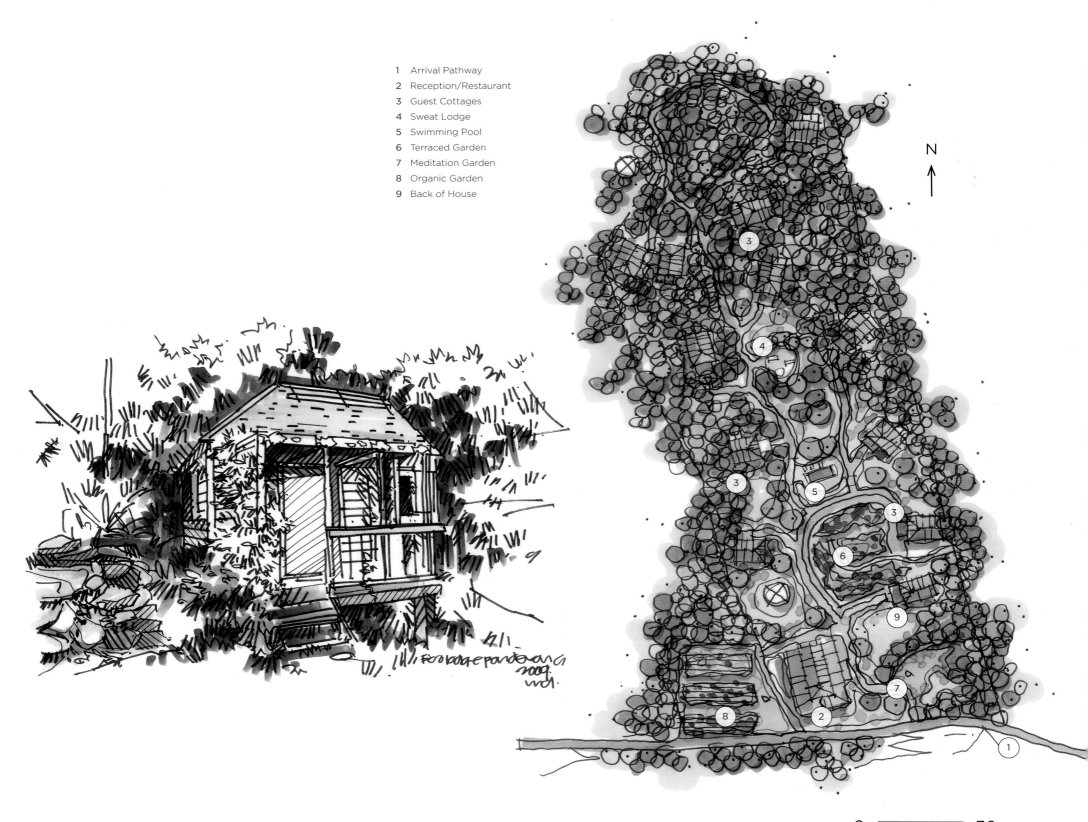

0 ⸺ 30m

The high-altitude Caribbean island of Saba has fifteen hundred residents, four towns, one road, ten cabbies, and no traffic lights. Despite its low profile, the island is world-renowned for its diving sites—ocean depths plummet more than 1,000 feet within a half mile from shore. Named for the Arawak word *siba*, which means "rock," Saba may be better known to cinephiles as Skull Island, the hardscrabble island featured in the original *King Kong*. And while the island is a 13 square kilometer (5 square mile) dormant volcano, locals simply know it as the "mountain that meets the sea." With sparse amenities, the real focus of Saba is on nature. Countless trails wind in and out of Saba National Park and a varied environment of lush rain forest canopy, shoreline, and rocky bluffs is home to exotic species of flora and fauna.

Located at the edge of the rain forest, Ecolodge Rendez-vous is an enclave of twelve solar-powered cottages. Family owned and operated, it is more than an exotic retreat; it is a place where guests are literally welcomed into the family fold. Husband Tom Van't Hof is one of the cofounders of the Saba Conservation Foundation and brings his several years' worth of preservation experience to Ecolodge Rendez-vous. Wife Heleen Cornet takes care of reservations and e-mail correspondences. Son Bernt is the lodge's chef, who prepares inspired dishes every night using food from the organic on-site garden. Dana, Bernt's wife, serves lunches and manages the hotel. While the Van't Hof family members add a distinctly personal flair to the lodge, they are just as passionate about its nuts and bolts as they are about its flourishes.

What is artsy about Ecolodge Rendez-vous is the fact that each cottage is designed and decorated by Heleen, a professional artist, according to a specific floral or faunal theme. Walls, wardrobes, and ceilings all become murals under Heleen's creative touch. As resident artist, her handiwork can

be seen on everything from the lodge's signs and placemats to the village café walls. Ecolodge Rendez-vous is an exemplary case of art as architecture.

During construction of the lodge, every effort was made to use ecofriendly and recycled materials like Trex Wood-Polymer, which is manufactured from reclaimed plastic and wood waste. The lodge's siding is made from HardiPlank, a product made of cement, sand, and recycled paper. Most cottages use Sealand low-flush toilets connected to SunMar nonelectrical composting units, producing odorless and pathogen-free compost. Water conservation is an issue on the island, and the lodge collects rainwater for reuse via solar panels and a 2.4 meter (8 foot) deep pump that moves the water to an upper cistern. The water is then gravity-fed throughout the cottages and restaurant. Gray water goes directly into the soil.

With a plunge pool hidden among papaya trees, and no access to radios, television, or telephones, guests can peacefully drop in and drop out, and rediscover a sense of self and a way of life harmoniously in touch with nature.

CUISINE: Considered one of the best restaurants on the island—homemade tropical ice cream, anyone?—the Rainforest Restaurant features Indonesian-themed nights and slideshows of hikes, presented by co-owner Tom Van't Hof. Additionally, 70 percent of the vegetables served in the restaurant and all herbs are organically grown on-site, ensuring the freshest ingredients possible.

ACTIVITIES: A volcanic-rock sweat lodge, complete with a modest yet exhilarating two-person cold plunge and hot tub, heated by a *chofu* (a Japanese wood stove) suffice as the on-site spa.

Previous spread: The lodge, in situ, on Saba Island, known colloquially as the "Unspoiled Queen." This page, top: Typical guest cottage designed and artfully painted by owner Heleen Cornet. Center: Local villager carrying mountain grass down to the village. Bottom: The restaurant is a local favorite, especially when owner Tom Van't Hof makes his presentations.

NIHIWATU

SUMBA ISLAND, INDONESIA

DATE OPENED
2001, with new facilities to come

OWNERS
Claude and Petra Graves

ENVIRONMENTAL PLANNER
HM Design (United States)

LANDSCAPE ARCHITECTS (NEW MASTER PLAN)
HM Design (United States) and 40 North (Costa Rica)

ARCHITECTS (FOR NEW FACILITIES)
Paul Pholeros (Australia), Simón Vélez (Colombia),
HM Design (United States)

FURNITURE DESIGN (FOR NEW FACILITIES)
Marcelo Villegas (Colombia)

Nihiwatu consists of 177 hectares (438 acres) of tropical forest, rice terraces, and sweeping grasslands that wrap around a 2.5 kilometer (1.5 mile) long crescent of white sand beach. The beach itself is buffeted on both ends by tall cliffs, making Nihiwatu a haven of exclusivity among this unspoiled region of the Indonesian archipelago. While the setting is remarkable, Nihiwatu's locally inspired architectural design rivals the lush beauty of the natural surroundings. Hand built by Indonesian craftsmen using local and recycled materials, such as teak and alang-alang grass, each of the seven thatched-roof bungalows and three two-bedroom villas has balcony views to the ocean and expansive glass walls that welcome the outdoors in. Coupled with these facts, no trees were cut during construction, the lodge has reforestation and reef-monitoring programs, a new biodiesel (coconut) factory that makes 270 liters (67 gallons) of biodiesel a day, and 0.8 hectare (2 acres) of land that is being organically farmed.

Owners Claude and Petra Graves have creatively used the artistic elements of the local Sumbanese culture to build an architecture of context at Nihiwatu. For example, intricately carved timber columns were retrieved from abandoned local houses and used in the reception and presidential villa pavilions. In Sumbanese culture, the four main wooden posts supporting the house from its foot to the top are closely associated with the rituals of ancestor worship. At Nihiwatu, wooden columns also become garden sculptures and are placed strategically at the arrival court. Local stone and wood sculptures are also placed carefully along pathways and ritual ornaments like masks and cattle horns are either displayed on walls or creatively turned into door handles. Renowned local Sumbanese ikat blankets adorn several of the important walls at Nihiwatu. Textiles in Sumba have always functioned as an indication of status and a means of ritual exchange. Each one of the lodge buildings have Sumbanese symbolic art and the villas are built with tall peaked roofs that are topped with a

Previous spread: The lodge, in situ, along one of Indonesia's premier beachfronts. Opposite, clockwise from top left: Art or architecture? Architectural detailing of a thatched wall; The presidential villa offers complete solitude in an idyllic tropical setting; The presidential villa lounge and dining area offers an impressive vista of the sea; Local villagers parading their traditional costumes; Guest rooms are decorated in contemporary Indonesian style. This page: The thatched-roof reception building is hand-built by local craftsmen using local materials. Top right: Sketch by Hitesh Mehta.

This page: Detail, hand-carved pillar.
Sketch by Marcelo Villegas.
Opposite page: Site plan by Matt Flynn.

projecting wooden beam at both ends that holds a male and a female figure made out of carved wood or bound grass—another local art form that becomes architecture at Nihiwatu.

Nihiwatu isn't simply good-looking; it's also incredibly good-hearted. The Graveses cofounded the Sumba Foundation, a nonprofit organization set up to follow through on three major initiatives: health, education, and clean water, and to date it has raised more than $1.6 million, with more than a third of that figure provided by lodge guests. Simply by distributing mosquito netting, the Sumba Foundation has successfully lowered the malaria rate in children under five from 62 percent to 10 percent. The Foundation has also built forty-seven deepwater wells that supply potable water for over eleven thousand neighboring Sumbanese. By providing local villagers access to education, health care, and clinics, along with a comprehensive team of health care professionals to assist in educational programs, Nihiwatu is living proof that ecotourism can support long-term humanitarian aid efforts. With a plan to expand to sixteen villas and three rental-pool executive villas,

and to transfer total ownership to the Sumba Foundation, this ecolodge may point the way for a successful balance of power among locals, tourists, and profits alike.

CUISINE: A locally trained chef prepares fusion dishes with organically sourced ingredients. The dining area is picture-perfect. Sweeping views of the ocean set a scenic backdrop for a memorable experience. Before dinner, most guests gather around the bar for customary tropical cocktails and snacks.

ACTIVITIES: The ecolodge is famous among surfers for the perfect left-hander wave that breaks off its beach. Besides surfing, there is an array of other activities: horseback riding along the beach; rain forest trekking to the Wanukaka Valley spring-fed waterfall; visiting local schools, markets, health clinics; diving; snorkeling; and partaking in the wellness center for yoga, massage therapy, and pilates. For a particularly memorable afternoon, visit one of the nearby Sumbanese villages for an authentic cultural experience.

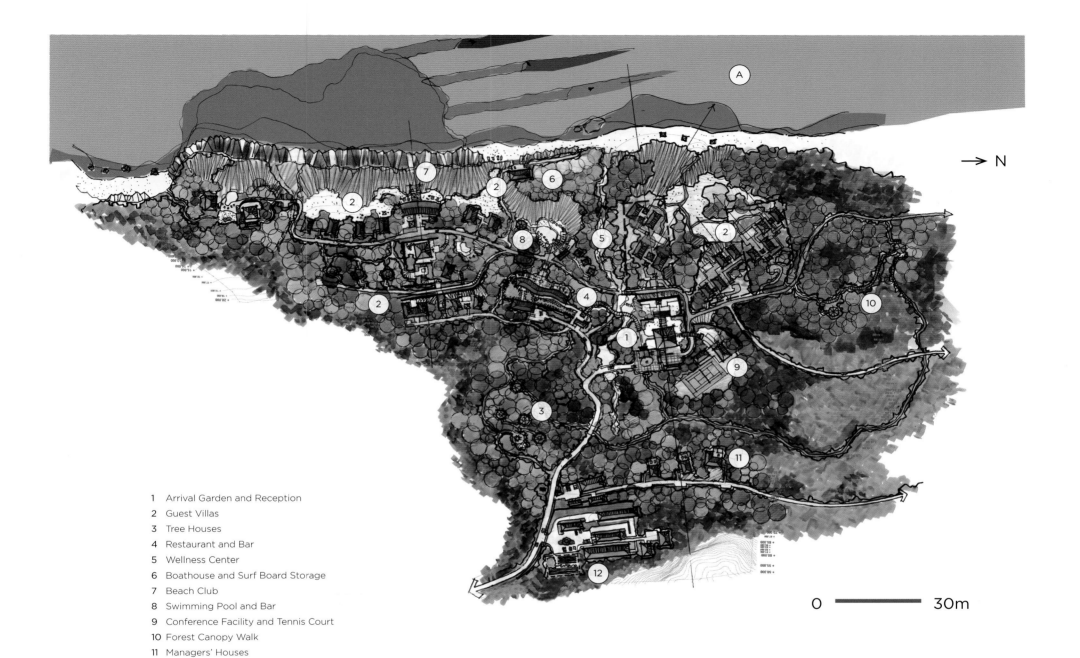

1 Arrival Garden and Reception
2 Guest Villas
3 Tree Houses
4 Restaurant and Bar
5 Wellness Center
6 Boathouse and Surf Board Storage
7 Beach Club
8 Swimming Pool and Bar
9 Conference Facility and Tennis Court
10 Forest Canopy Walk
11 Managers' Houses
12 Back of House

_____

A Indian Ocean

→ N

0 ▬▬▬▬ 30m

INTERPRETATION PROGRAMS

Interpretation programs are one of the cornerstones of all ecolodge operations, with conservation and local community benefits being the other two. Indeed, interpretation programs are chief among the identifying characteristics that separate an ecolodge from traditional lodging. The ecolodges showcased in this chapter all have established interpretation programs and use innovative and varied interpretative methods to expose visitors to concepts related to the ecolodge's setting, biology, local communities, and operations. These methods might include medicinal and guided nature walks, live local music and dance, wildlife photography, videography, local village walks, and hands-on crafts such as weaving and clay pottery. In other words, the ecolodges presented here provide the best opportunities for visitors to experience or discover certain plants, animals, archaeological ruins, or cultural aspects of the area in a way that does not ultimately damage the sustainability of the facility or the region.

One thing only I know,
and that is that I know nothing.
—Socrates

PHINDA FOREST LODGE

KWAZULU-NATAL, SOUTH AFRICA

DATE COMPLETED
1994

OWNER
&Beyond

ARCHITECT
Ridler Shepherd Low (South Africa)

INTERIOR DESIGN
Chris Brown (South Africa)

dyllically situated 30 kilometers (19 miles) due west of the white-fringed beaches of the Indian Ocean and bordering the Greater St. Lucia Wetland Park (UNESCO World Heritage Site), Phinda Forest Lodge lies in Phinda Private Game Reserve. The reserve is managed by &Beyond, but 40 percent of the land is owned by the adjacent Makasa and Mnqobokazi Zulu communities. Phinda Forest Lodge takes its name from the surrounding Sand Forest, a unique ecological habitat that occupies less than 1 percent of Africa's land surface, and is home to some of the world's most rarified and restricted-range species, including the red duiker, the suni, the African wood owl, and the mamba swordtail butterfly.

In the world of safari ecolodges, Phinda Forest Lodge's interpretation programs are without peer. Their research and interpretation oriented safaris are conducted by a knowledgeable head guide, and include birding, bush skills academy, leopard research, photography, rhino capture and research, tracking, and walking safaris. The lodge also has nine

nature guides and eleven local Zulu trackers, who impart an incomparable wealth of knowledge, personally researched and experienced, about the local habitats and ecology. Detailed and well-illustrated in-house "guide" booklets prepared by &Beyond adorn the shelf in every guest accommodation: the ecologist's modern-day Gideon Bible, as it were.

Modern in design yet built with an emphasis toward conservationism, the lodge itself is comprised of sixteen spacious, hand-built, glass-encased luxury suites. Built on stilts within a grove of torchwood trees, the suites appear to float between the Sand Forest floor and the tree canopy. Only twelve trees were cut during construction; all materials were carried by hand through the forest, foundations were all hand dug, and local construction crews worked on two suites at a time to lessen the environmental impact. The overall atmosphere of Phinda Forest Lodge is Zulu Zen. An expansive viewing deck and infinity pool provide the ultimate setting for enjoying the panoramic views of the game-filled savannah

Previous spread: The lodge is located in the dry sand forest of Phinda Private Game Reserve. Opposite, clockwise from top left: A breakfast sampling of tropical treats; Guest suite bathrooms, with views into the forest, are constructed mainly of natural materials, including locally sourced slate; Designed to leave a light footprint, the lodge's suites were constructed around the trees; Completely glass enclosed, the bedrooms exude a Zulu Zen sensibility. This page, left and right: Each hand-crafted stilted suite is a combination of glass, wood, and minimalist design.

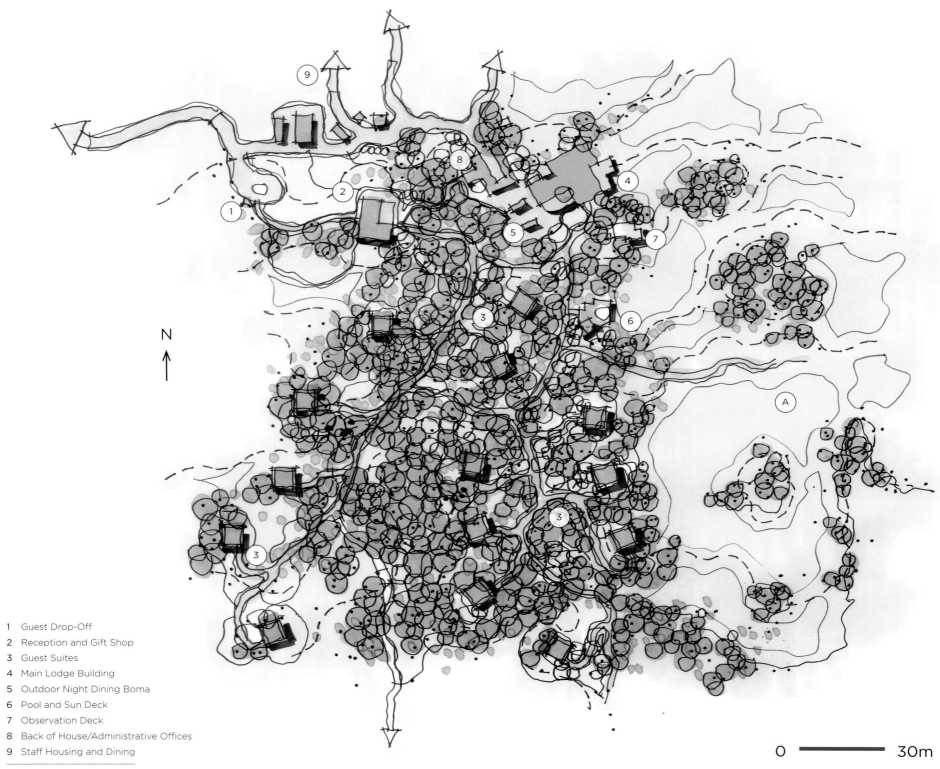

1 Guest Drop-Off
2 Reception and Gift Shop
3 Guest Suites
4 Main Lodge Building
5 Outdoor Night Dining Boma
6 Pool and Sun Deck
7 Observation Deck
8 Back of House/Administrative Offices
9 Staff Housing and Dining

A Phinda Private Game Reserve

N

0 ▬▬▬▬▬ 30m

woodlands. The all-glass suites are minimalist, yet furnished with colorful fabrics and Zulu artifacts. While the setting (both inside and out) is inspired, Phinda's comprehensive interpretation programs make it one of South Africa's most rarified safari lodges.

CUISINE: Guests with special dietary needs are well taken care of by the skillful cooking staff. There are also several dining venues to choose from: the open-air decks in each villa for an intimate experience, the view deck, and the beautifully designed boma where a campfire and starlit skies create a romantic atmosphere.

ACTIVITIES: Every manner of safari is possible at Phinda: game drives, interpretive bush walks, Mzinene River canoeing. For those adventurers who crave an additional jolt of adrenaline, there's deep-sea diving safaris, Isikolethu cultural tours, and black rhino tracking excursions, to name just a few.

This page, left: Secluded by sand forest habitat, the ecolodge is a tucked-away gem; Above, top: The African leopard is the crowning glory of game-drive interpretive experiences at Phinda. Center: Open to the elements, the dining room breakfast deck welcomes the outdoors. Bottom: The savannah plains combined with forest habitat make for exciting interpretive safari excursions.

WILDERNESS LODGE ARTHUR'S PASS

SOUTH ISLAND, NEW ZEALAND

DATE COMPLETED
1996

OWNERS
McSweeney and Jarman Families

ARCHITECT
Gary Hopkinson (New Zealand)

On the scenic western side of South Island, New Zealand, surrounded by Arthur's Pass National Park, is the family-owned and operated Wilderness Lodge Arthur's Pass. Although the McSweeney and Jarman families can trace their New Zealand farming ancestry back to 1860, the lodge itself was built in 1996, by west coast wilderness architect Gary Hopkinson. Predominately featuring sustainably harvested local wood, stone, and corrugated iron, the award-winning twenty-four-room lodge effortlessly blends into its natural surroundings of mountain beech forest. Originally operated as a sheep farm, husband-and-wife team and managing directors Dr. Gerry McSweeney and Ann Saunders have remained true to the land: Wilderness Lodge Arthur's Pass is still, to this day, a working sheep farm and guests are encouraged to visit the merino sheep at the sheep station.

The lodge is at the forefront in interpretation programming. Every day, the naturalist guides led by Gerry McSweeney offer two activities that are each about an hour long and are included in the lodge tariff. Guests can learn about beech forests and New Zealand's smallest bird, discover thorn forests, and look for one of the world's smartest animals, the kea parrot. Astronomy walks introduce guests to the Southern Cross and night sky. The naturalist guides help guests learn about high-country life and explore nature in this special place the first Māori visitors called Te Ko Awa a Aniwaniwa (Valley of the Mother of the Rainbows). The lodge has also established a network of trails 30 kilometers (20 miles) in length, and guests can partake in self-guided walks using detailed maps and manuals provided by the lodge. Lodge guests can also book in advance for a special day of nature discovery with their own exclusive nature guide. The most interpretive experience is without a doubt with Gerry McSweeney, who is an ecologist by profession. His guided walks through the tussock lands, wetlands, and beech forest or trekking in the upper Otira Valley to find exquisite white cups of *Ranunculus lyallii*, the giant Mt. Cook buttercup, are one-of-a-kind excursions.

Previous spread: The lodge, in the foreground, surrounded by Arthur's Pass National Park. Opposite, clockwise from top left: With its clean architectural lines, the ecolodge is a bastion for modern comfort; A stunning waterfall, just one of several wilderness sites to discover; Living areas are simply decorated and feature wood, concrete, and corrugated iron; The ecolodge is designed to blend in with the surroundings. This page: Breathtaking early morning view of the New Zealand landscape.

Above, top: Owner and renowned New Zealand ecologist gives a talk on the area's flora and fauna. Above: The ecolodge is also a working merino sheep farm. Right: Buffered by beech forest and tussock clearings, the ecolodge delivers a one-of-a-kind experience.

Over the years, McSweeney and Saunders have extended their sense of passion into various conservation programs and the lodge is now surrounded by its own 2,400 hectare (5,930 acre) nature reserve. Lodge-based conservation efforts include landscaping with only native plants, passive solar techniques such as the use of low-e double-glazed windows, low-flow showerheads using gravity spring-fed medium pressure, and compact fluorescent light fittings. Having recently participated in a reforestation program of 1,215 hectares (3,000 acres) of property, reintroducing endangered plants such as mistletoe and native broom, and restoring wetlands on the property, the Wilderness Lodge Arthur's Pass is an acknowledged leader in South Island biodiversity conservation. The lodge may be at the heart of the Southern Alps, but it's the owners' commitment to preserving the land that gives the Wilderness Lodge Arthur's Pass heart.

CUISINE: The lodge's Mt. Rolleston Restaurant has a reputation of its own for serving up a selection of New Zealand's best dishes, like Black Doris Plum and Kumara (sweet potato). The menu changes daily depending on the freshness of the ingredients, and includes a comprehensive wine menu.

ATTRACTIONS: Guests can canoe along Lake Pearson or Lake Sarah and look for crested grebe, scaup, paradise ducks, and other wetland birds. The serene Māori rock landscape of neighboring Kura Tawhiti (Castle Hill) provides a meditative respite, while the Franz Josef and Fox glaciers are the perfect settings for an adventure-filled afternoon.

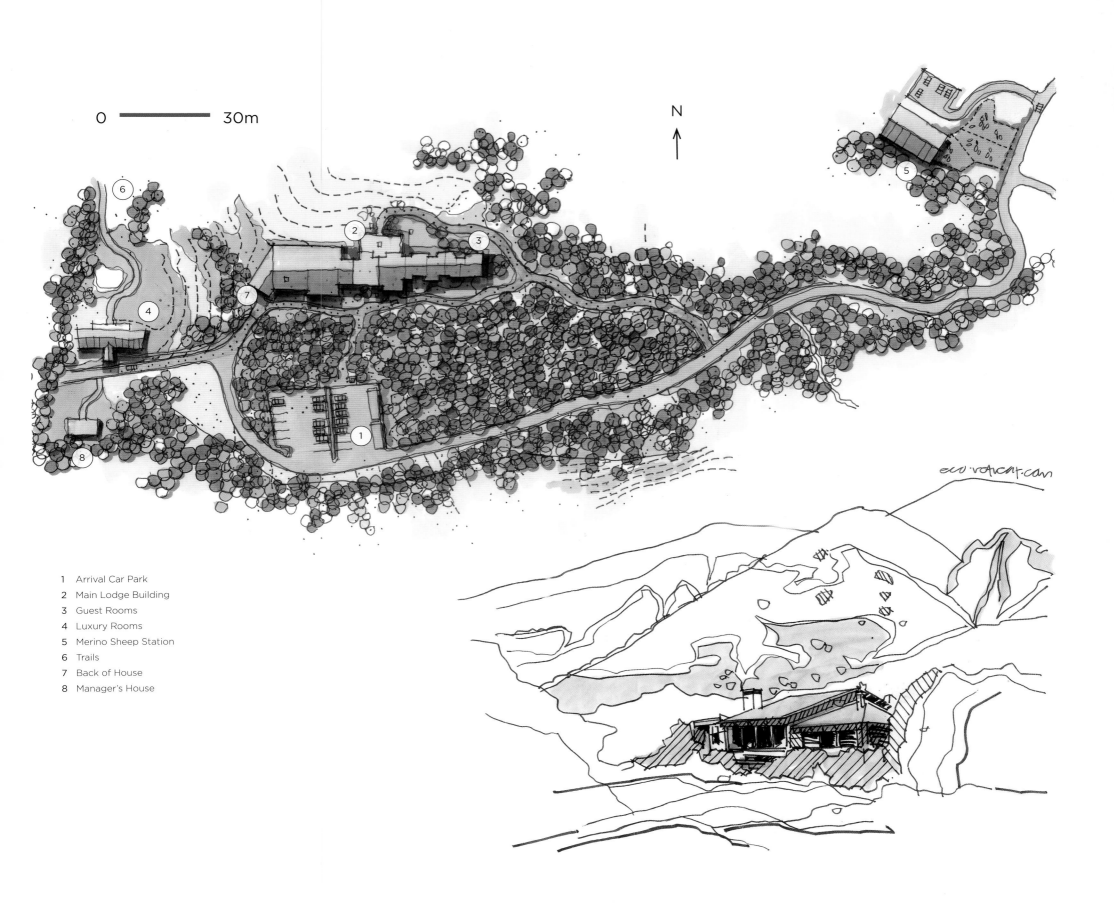

0 ⟞————⟝ 30m

N ↑

eco·vatican·com

1 Arrival Car Park
2 Main Lodge Building
3 Guest Rooms
4 Luxury Rooms
5 Merino Sheep Station
6 Trails
7 Back of House
8 Manager's House

BASECAMP MAASAI MARA
KOYIAKI GROUP RANCH, KENYA

DATE COMPLETED
1998

OWNER
Basecamp Explorer

Born of a unique vision—to help diverse peoples work together, protect biodiversity and culture, and promote the sustainable use of the environment—Basecamp Maasai Mara is located just outside the Maasai Mara Game Reserve area of southwestern Kenya. Besides its breathtaking panoramic views of endless savannah, escarpments, and sky, the Maasai Mara Game Reserve (together with adjoining Serengeti National Park) boasts the most diverse and greatest concentration of large mammals in the world. In fact, during July and August the reserve hosts the so-called Greatest Show on Earth. It is one of the largest migrations of large animals, including wildebeest and zebra and their accompanying predators: lions, cheetahs, crocodiles, leopards, jackals, and hyenas. During off-season from the planet's ultimate wildlife-watching opportunity, the reserve is also a bird-watching haven and home to several other notable mammal species, including the endangered black rhino, elephant, hippo, and Cape buffalo, among others. As if

this weren't enough to make a stay in the Mara unforgettable, Basecamp Maasai Mara provides fifteen environmentally and socially friendly rustic, thatched-roofed "tented" villas, each with its own private veranda overlooking the Talek River and the game reserve, which comfortably situate guests within the dramatic natural surroundings. The viewing deck offers spectacular views of the sun setting over the Burrungat savannah plains.

Basecamp Maasai Mara delivers a truly unique interpretive and transformative experience. No matter which of the camp's many activities guests choose to partake in—from a Maasai guided traditional medicine plant walk to an authentic Maasai village tour to a guided wildlife safari—chances are that the views of the incredible Mara vista, punctuated by the surrounding savannah sounds, will inspire anyone to take a walk on the wild side. To further enlighten guests, all trees in the camp are identified by both their Latin and Maa (local language) names. And Basecamp Maasai

Previous spread: The lodge, in situ, on the banks of the Talek River, Maasai Mara. Opposite page, clockwise from top left: The lodge is located in the Koiyaki Maasai Community Group Ranch, which borders the Maasai Mara Game Reserve; Interpretive activities include Maasai-guided safari tours on foot; A Mara cheetah on a morning hunt; Nature is just outside the door; Charming interiors are all made from local materials and have strong Maasai themes. This page: The main lodge building comprises the lounge and upper deck, dining area, and bar.

Above: Guests at the ecolodge have the opportunity to partake in a truly authentic Maasai village experience.

guides also offer different interpretive activities for children. Among other hands-on experiences, children learn how to make bows and arrows, how to make footprint castings, and how to look for the tracks of wild animals.

One of the most impressive features of the Basecamp Maasai Mara is its community-based arts program with the Maasai women (Maasai Arts and Crafts Project), in which guests are able to visit at the camp with local Maasai artisans to watch art-in-the-making. A full 75 percent of the sales generated by the artisans' beadwork goes directly to the women who make the art; the remaining 25 percent goes toward art supplies. In addition to the Bead Project, the camp has also produced a one-of-a-kind Maasai audio CD to preserve and document the songs, tradition, culture, and stories of the Maasai in the Talek area so that they are available for future generations.

CUISINE: Chefs serve local Kenyan food like *irio*, *ugali*, and *chapati*, along with freshly baked bread, traditional Western lunches, bush breakfasts and dinners, which can be taken under the stars, weather permitting, or in the thatched roof dining hall.

ACTIVITIES: Activities include day and night game drives, nature walks outside the game reserve and in the group ranch, bird-watching, village tours, and balloon safaris.

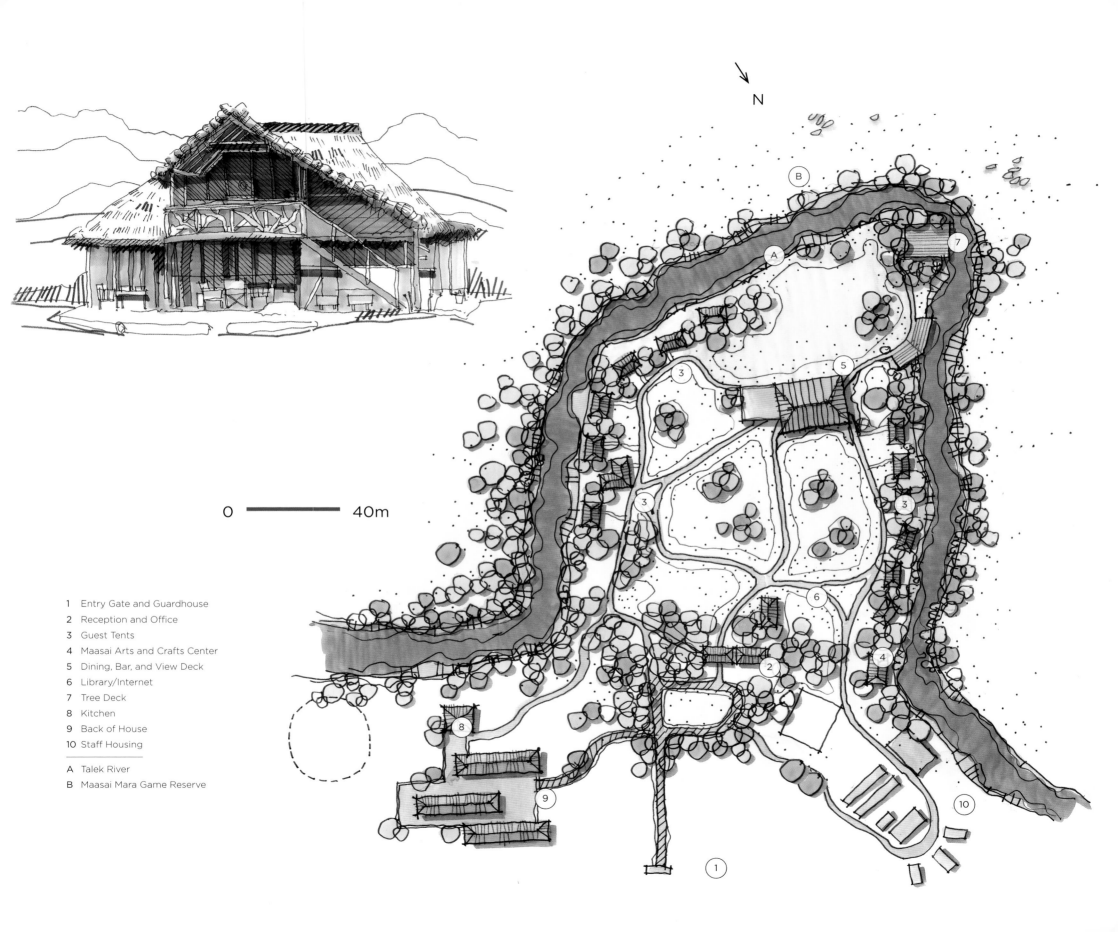

N

1   Entry Gate and Guardhouse
2   Reception and Office
3   Guest Tents
4   Maasai Arts and Crafts Center
5   Dining, Bar, and View Deck
6   Library/Internet
7   Tree Deck
8   Kitchen
9   Back of House
10 Staff Housing

—————————————

A   Talek River
B   Maasai Mara Game Reserve

0 ━━━━━━ 40m

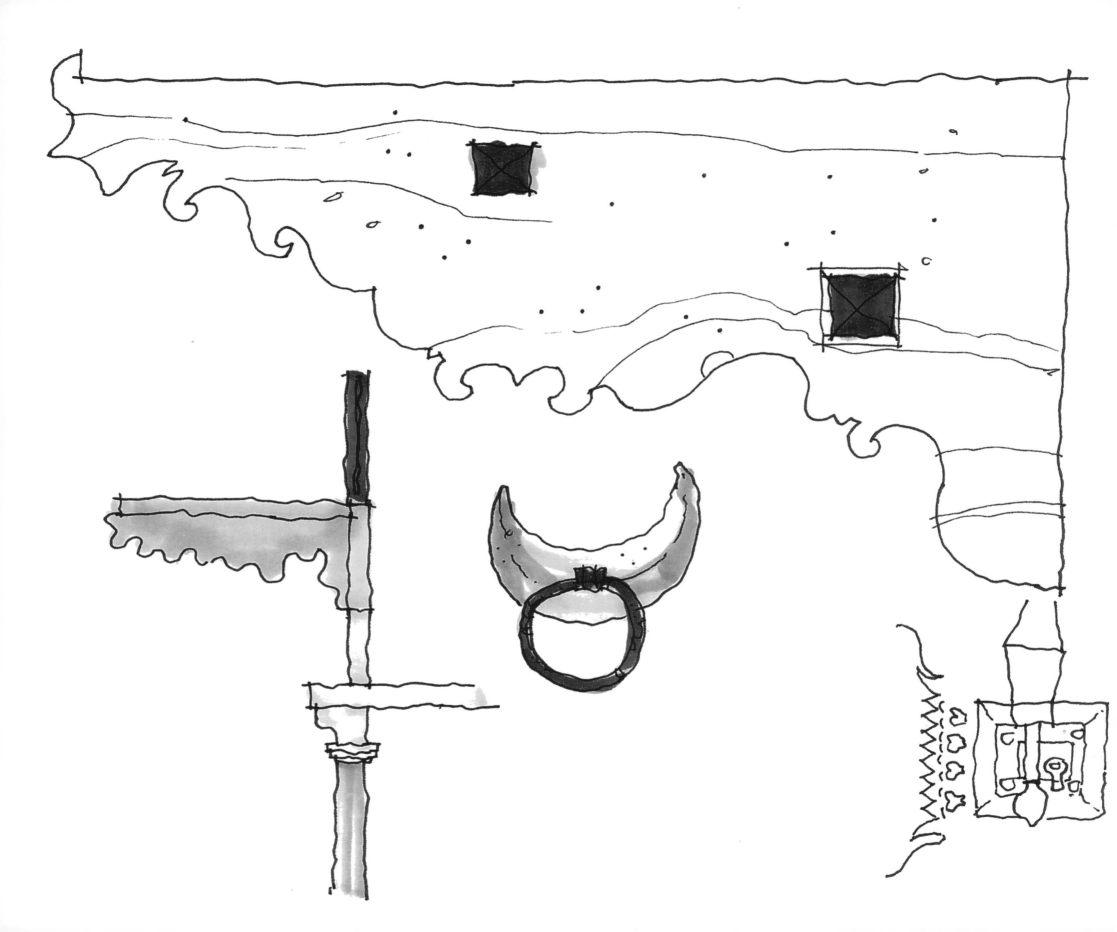

REUSE AND RECYCLE

In the context of *Authentic Ecolodges*, recycle and reuse refer to an approach where existing and abandoned buildings have been given new life by visionary ecolodge owners. In each of the ecolodges presented here, old buildings were given new life through creative reusing and recycling of materials, building parts, and equipment. Some instances involve the refurbishment and conversion of existing buildings into an ecolodge complete with modern kitchens, dining and lounge areas, and guest villas, while other instances include the transportation of abandoned buildings from local villages to the site of the ecolodge, where they are then converted to guest housing.

We have a moral responsibility to protect the earth and ensure that our children and grandchildren have a healthy and sustainable environment in which to live.
—Jim Clyburn

COCONUT LAGOON

KERALA, INDIA

DATE COMPLETED
1993

OWNERS
CGH Earth

VISIONARY PLANNER
Jose Dominic (India)

MASTER WOOD CRAFTSMAN
Bhaskaran Assari (India)

Accessible only by boat, Coconut Lagoon is hidden among the palm trees on the eastern shore of Lake Vembanad, at Kumarakom, the heart of the "backwaters" of Kerala. The lodge is set on an abandoned coconut plantation and not only represents an innovative, highly sustainable model for ecofriendly destinations, but is also designed to give visitors authentic insight into the local Kuttanad (meaning "land of the short people") life. As such, Coconut Lagoon remains true to its environment, synthesizing modern sustainability techniques with the area's cultural history. While most of the world's authentic ecolodges have recycling and reuse programs in place, Coconut Lagoon takes this one step further, having constructed both the reception building and the lodge's restaurant from reassembled parts of nineteenth-century traditional *nalukettu* and *ettukettu* (eight rooms with two central courtyards) houses. The results are not only visually stunning, but also genuinely reflect the lodge's commitment to its cultural roots and architectural heritage.

Village craftspeople were contracted to restore the work of their forefathers. Abandoned *therawads* (family homes) were dismantled piece by piece and transported to the Coconut Lagoon site to create a one-of-a-kind ecolodge experience. The local carpenters practiced the Ayurvedic science of carpentry called Thatchu Shastra: During construction, no nails were used and environmentally friendly materials—reused *anjali* wood, reused clay tiles for the roof and floors, and bamboo screens—were utilized wherever possible. The lodge itself is crisscrossed with canals and footbridges that lead to rustic yet modern-looking white bungalows and two-story mansions, a few of which date back to the early 1700s. The lodge's restaurant utilizes a traditional courtyard design—that of a long corridor—with a twist. The sides of the corridor are slatted, providing not only fresh air but also shelter from the harsh summer light.

From waste-water recycling to plastics disposal, from sewage treatment to the avoidance of all chemical pesticides, Coconut Lagoon prides itself on its water resourcing,

Previous spread: The lodge, in situ, along the shores of Vembanad, the longest lake in India. Opposite: The *ettukettu*-inspired landscape architecture of the restaurant. Water is one of the lodge's defining architectural elements. This page, left: Tiled-roof buildings echo the old-world graciousness of feudal Kerala. Above: Village craftsmen expertly constructed the ecolodge to be as beautiful as it is ecologically sound.

227

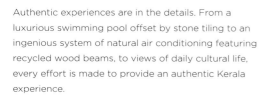

Authentic experiences are in the details. From a luxurious swimming pool offset by stone tiling to an ingenious system of natural air conditioning featuring recycled wood beams, to views of daily cultural life, every effort is made to provide an authentic Kerala experience.

conservation, and recycling efforts. To this end, a reverse osmosis river plant channels 2,000 liters (440 gallons) of water per hour and filters approximately 50,000,000 liters (11 million gallons) of rainwater, which is harvested and stored in a pond; composting heaps are left in the open (and not out of mind); the biogas facility converts natural and plant waste into clean, burnable fuel; and organic rice farming is promoted, minimizing the environmental impact. Many of Coconut Lagoon's techniques have been adopted in the area, making the Vembanad Lake cleaner and greener for generations to come.

The spirit of Kerala is alive and well at Coconut Lagoon. From its canals and organic rice paddies to innovative design and comprehensive recycling programs, the lodge inspires thoughtful contemplation, whether enjoying its pristine scenic views or partaking in any one of its comprehensive activities.

CUISINE: Sample some authentic Kerala Malabari food as well as south Indian delicacies, like *idly-sambhar* and *dhosa*, laid out in a sumptuous buffet in the lodge's beautiful dining room, which dates from 1863. The menu also features Ayurvedic drinks and foods that have specific restorative, digestive, or cooling effects. Taste these in combination with fresh organic vegetables, locally harvested coconut water, and, of course, the myriad spices that form the backbone of Indian cooking.

ACTIVITIES: Learn how to peel cinnamon, pick up a recipe at one of the lodge's cooking classes, or take a bullock cart ride. Guests of Coconut Lagoon are also invited to take village walks and sunset cruises, go canoeing and kayaking, and take yoga and meditation classes. Beyond this, there is an array of additional excursions, including tours of Kumarakom Sanctuary—the local bird sanctuary—and the hotel's open-air butterfly garden, home to ninety-three species of butterflies and forty-five species of dragonfly. The area surrounding the Vembanad Lake is a treasure trove for naturalists with a plethora of plant and animal species, including fifty-three species of fish.

→ N

1   Arrival Boat Dock
2   Reception and Offices
3   Guest Rooms
4   Guest Villas
5   Lounge/Bar
6   Restaurant
7   Ayurvedic Center/Yoga Pavilion
8   Swimming Pool
9   Gift Shop
10 Organic Rice Paddy
11 Interpretation Center
12 Back of House

A   Vembanad Lake
B   Kavanar River
C   Kumarakom Bird Sanctuary

0   40m

CANOPY TOWER

SOBERANÌA NATIONAL PARK, PANAMA

DATE COMPLETED
1999

OWNER
Raul Arias de Para (Panama)

VISIONARY AND IMPLEMENTATION
Raul Arias de Para

Previous spread: The lodge, in situ, towering over the forest canopy. Opposite: The down-to-earth restaurant, in one of the tower's top two floors, has exposed, reused ceiling steel beams. This page: The ecolodge's geotangent dome makes the perfect perch to keep an eye on the nearly 380 species of birds in adjacent forest trees.

Originally built in 1965 by the U.S. Air Force as a radar station and used until 1995 to detect airplanes suspected of carrying drugs from South America, Canopy Tower is perched 275 meters (900 feet) above sea level, gracing visitors with unparalleled views of the Panama Canal and the surrounding tropical rain forest. Nestled in the heart of Soberanìa National Park, Canopy Tower is a prime lookout point from which to see the 283 species of birds—motmots, toucans, and fruit crows, among others—that call the treetops home, making it the region's premier bird-watching spot. The National Park also hosts an abundance of other species, including the agouti, ocelot, three-toed sloth, howler monkey, jaguarundi, and nine-banded armadillo. While location can be everything—and Canopy Towers does not disappoint in this regard—ecological solidarity with the natural surroundings is paramount when creating a genuine ecolodge. With its creative approach to sustainable construction and adaptive transformation, Canopy Towers represents the height of visionary "extreme makeover" thinking.

Canopy Tower is, without doubt, one of the best authentic ecolodge examples in the world of architectural "recycle and reuse." Though it's no easy task to transform a military tower into an ecological haven, Canopy Towers controlled the impact made on the earth in part by using a maximum of only five to ten people at a time to work on the site. Everything was steel bolted, not welded, and no large construction machines, like Caterpillars, were used. The interiors of the lodge utilize an abundance of environmentally friendly materials, including teak from a local plantation. The reception desk is made from old canal houses and many of the doors and windows as well as the marble (for use in the bathrooms) are from the owner's apartment, which not only illustrates his personal commitment to the lodge but also imbues it with a homey feel.

The tower itself consists of four levels and a ground floor, which contains the reception, interpretive area, and

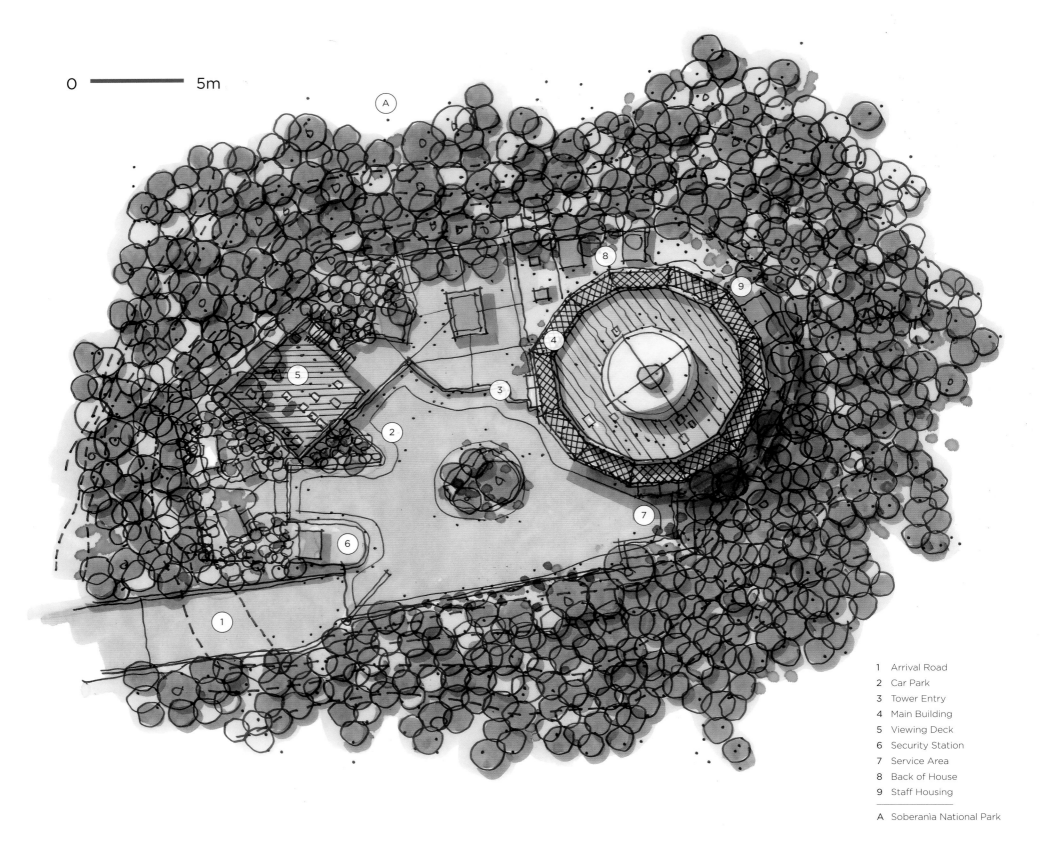

0 ▬▬▬▬▬ 5m

1   Arrival Road
2   Car Park
3   Tower Entry
4   Main Building
5   Viewing Deck
6   Security Station
7   Service Area
8   Back of House
9   Staff Housing

A   Soberanìa National Park

souvenir shop. The observation deck is 15 meters (50 feet) off the ground and graced with a breathtaking, 360-degree view of the national park, the Panama Canal, Panama City, and the Pacific Ocean. The third level is the community floor, with the dining room, kitchen, living room, and library, while the remaining levels are dedicated to guest bedrooms and suites, including the Blue Cotinga Suite with a diaphanous canopy bed, plantation wood furniture, and an outdoor veranda swing. Well-designed amenities and an unbelievable location certainly make Canopy Towers comfortable and irresistibly beautiful, but it is the lodge's intense commitment to conservation, bird-watching programs, and the local staff that elevates it above the rest of Panamanian lodges.

The longtime staff of Canopy Towers is 100 percent Panamanian. (The lodge had, in the early days, employed several of the area's poachers as bird guides in an effort to change the practice of poaching.) On some evenings, the lodge hosts presentations, with information on everything from the environment and its impact on the birds' natural habitat to the best ways of seeing elusive species. There are never more than eight people to one guide, ensuring a uniquely intimate and comprehensive tour every time. The ecolodge has ten bird-watching tours near the site and over

ten historical and cultural tours outside the park. With the possibility of observing rare, endangered birds and three-toed sloths from the bedrooms, Canopy Towers truly is an ecolodge with a view, one that leaves its guests with indelible memories rarely found in the Americas.

CUISINE: The owner's sister, Cuquita Arias (a Panamanian celebrity chef), created the haute cuisine menu for Canopy Towers, which guarantees healthy, home-cooked meals served buffet style. There are also plenty of vegetables, fresh fruits, nuts, and several veggie and vegan dishes made with tofu, soy products, and other cruelty-free ingredients.

ACTIVITIES: With thirteen different birding tours that range from the simple (birding around the lodge) to the exotic (birding on a boat in the Panama Canal) Canopy Towers is a true haven for bird enthusiasts and anyone interested in viewing forest wildlife in its natural habitat. For nonbirders, guided tours of local monuments, museums, Panama City, as well as a visit to the San Blas Islands—home to the indigenous Kuna peoples—are available.

KASBAH DU TOUBKAL

IMLIL, MOROCCO

DATE COMPLETED
1995

OWNER
Discover Ltd.

ARCHITECT
John Bothamley (England)

A mountain retreat perched in the High Atlas and at the base of 4,165 meter (13,665 foot) Jbel Toubkal, North Africa's highest mountain, Kasbah du Toubkal provides a genuine taste of Moroccan village life. Located within the tiny village of Achein, the building was once the private home of the Caid Souktani, a brutal Berber feudal ruler, who was unseated with Morocco's independence in 1956. The heavily fortified residence got a makeover in the early 1990s and today is a striking example of Moroccan architecture and style. Complete with male and female hammams (the traditional Arab communal bathhouse) and managed by local Berber couple Hajj Maurice and wife Hajja Arkia, the Kasbah is more of a Berber hospitality center than a lodge. The local Berber staff treat every guest as an extension of their families. The sweeping views of the surrounding landscape—reddish brown mountains lush with green walnut groves and, in the distance, the rising snowcapped peaks of Mount Toubkal—are considered by some to be the best in North Africa. Savvy guests may recognize

the scenic vista as the backdrop to Martin Scorsese's 1997 film, *Kundun*. From its cinematic atmosphere to its dedication to a comprehensive architectural recycle-and-reuse program, it's clear that this is no ordinary lodge.

The brainchild of British brothers Mike and Chris McHugo, the rehabilitation of the residence ruin into a comfortable forty-nine-guest capacity lodge was carried out under the expert supervision of the locally born Omar Hajj Maurice. No power tools were used in the construction and restoration of Kasbah du Toubkal, and every attempt was made to retain many of the traditional building techniques and wood decorations of the local Berber community. Using all local labor, environmentally friendly building materials were brought on-site via mules: Stone is from neighboring hills and rivers, tiles are from Marrakech and Fez, and marble is from the southern desert.

The friendly staff give guests the unique opportunity to interact with the local people and culture. Mountain treks, led

Previous spread: The lodge, in situ, at the foot of the snow-covered Mount Toubkal. Opposite, clockwise from top: The restaurant's décor captures the flair and romance of old-world Morocco; Local staff member in the lodge reception; Moroccan spices on display in the local Asni market; Berber furnishings in the guest bedrooms are both simple and sophisticated. This page, left: Dun-colored exteriors effortlessly blend into the mountain landscape. Above: Entry court of the traditional hammam.

Above, top: Rows of houses, Tamatert village, an hour's walk from the Kasbah. Above: The ecolodge's idyllic entrance.

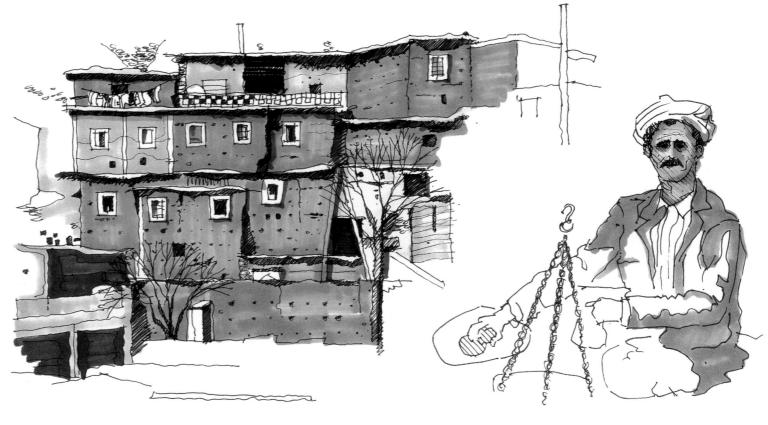

by trained Berber guides, encourage guests to fully immerse themselves in the Moroccan way of life. Indirect benefits to the wider community are fulfilled by a 5 percent surcharge added to all Kasbah services, the proceeds of which are passed on to the nearest large village association—the Association des Bassins d'Imlil—which manages daily operations such as rubbish removal, an ambulance service, community hammam, and provisions for accommodation in the Asni village for children to attend school, among other services.

Kasbah is the perfect synthesis of eco-conservancy and midlevel luxury. Springwater is resourced by gravity feeding, and each marble-tiled bathroom is equipped with biodegradable shampoos and soaps. With its comprehensive solid-waste management program, all plastic, cardboard, aluminum, and glass are sorted and sent 60 kilometers (37 miles) away to Marrakech to be reused and recycled, paper is burnt in the kitchen incinerator, and organic waste is fed to goats and cows. A modern-day Berber citadel blessed with

a healthy dose of ecoconsciousness, Kasbah provides a level of comfort, graciousness, and hospitality unrivaled in the area and uncommon in the rest of the world.

CUISINE: Traditional Moroccan cuisine is served for lunch and dinner. The cuisine of Morocco is a mix of Arab, Berber, Moorish, Middle Eastern, Mediterranean, and African influences. The vegetarian *tajine* is the specialty with aromatic vegetables, spices, and sauce.

ACTIVITIES: The Kasbah can be used as a base for climbing Mount Toubkal, combining it with a night's stay at its sister property, the new Toubkal Lodge. The local Berber village guided walk is the highlight of most guests' stays. There is also horseback riding, mule trekking, skiing on Mount Toubkal, and, of course, the relaxing steam baths in the hammam.

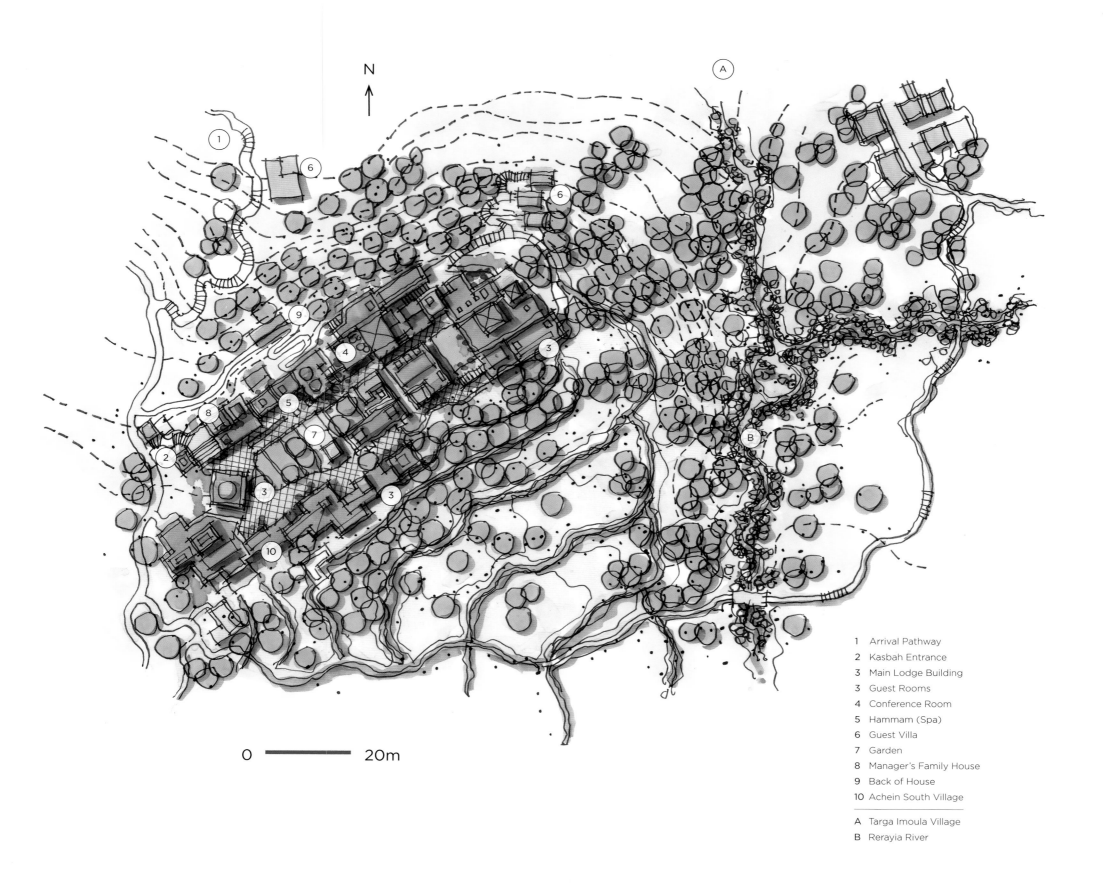

N

1 Arrival Pathway
2 Kasbah Entrance
3 Main Lodge Building
3 Guest Rooms
4 Conference Room
5 Hammam (Spa)
6 Guest Villa
7 Garden
8 Manager's Family House
9 Back of House
10 Achein South Village

A Targa Imoula Village
B Rerayia River

0 ━━━━━━━━ 20m

UNIQUE EXPERIENCES

There are certain authentic ecolodges in the world that provide experiences that are so unique that one cannot replicate them anywhere else on the planet. These lodges represent experiential travel at its best whereby guests return to their homes with indelible memories—and the wanderlust for return visits. This chapter showcases three ecolodges that offer transformative experiences leagues above the rest. These lodges not only capture the spirit and rhythm of the local culture, they are also located amid some of the world's most rarified property.

When one tugs at a single thing in nature, he finds it attached to the rest of the world.
—John Muir

JALMAN MEADOWS GER CAMP

KHAN KHENTI PROTECTED AREA, MONGOLIA

DATE COMPLETED
2000

OWNER
Nomadic Journeys (Sweden)

DESIGNER
Jan Wigsten (Sweden)

Previous spread: The lodge, in situ, its white-tented domes (laid in a cluster in the background) dotting the landscape of Khan Khenti Protected Area. Opposite: The tents are simply constructed yet beautiful in their simplicity. This page: Jalman Meadows is the perfect setting for a remote getaway.

Jalman Meadows Ger Camp lies in the Upper Tuul River Valley, serenely tucked away from the traffic lights and the hustle and bustle of Mongolian's capital city, Ulaanbaatar. The camp is hidden deep within the meadows of the Jalman Mountains, which rise and fall into soft peaks and plateaus, lush with greenery and alive with color during the fall season. After completing a three-and-a-half-hour drive northeast from Ulaanbaatar, guests arrive at an indistinct dirt road that leads to a small summit. Only then does Jalman Meadows Ger Camp come into full view, a sprawling compound dotted with fully collapsible white tents nestled against the stunning backdrop of a larch forest generously sprinkled with a colorful array of wildflowers. The camp itself is perched upland overlooking the Tuul River in the Khan Khenti Special Protected Area, a wilderness site three times the size of Yellowstone. Ideally situated amid one of the world's most inspired settings and with a maximum capacity of twenty guests, Jalman Meadows Ger Camp is not only an

exclusively intimate retreat, it also provides guests with a truly transformative experience.

The Tuul River is an integral resource to Jalman Meadows Ger Camp. Water from the river's tributary is hauled by yak cart to camp, where it is boiled and filtered for drinking. And while there is no filtration for shower water, the river acts as the perfect swimming hole for hot days or for cold dips while using the sauna. Rafting is a common activity, too. With an eye toward conservation, the camp employs a hybrid system of solar and wind for electricity. When the sun is bright and shining and the wind is strong, the camp benefits from a double dose of electrical energy. Candles are the prevalent sources of light, however. Built using environmentally friendly materials—a combination of felt, sheep, and goat wool for insulation, canvas for the tents' exteriors, and furniture built with wood from Central Mongolia—the camp is a model of sustainable deconstruction with a nomadic twist. The entire camp can literally be broken

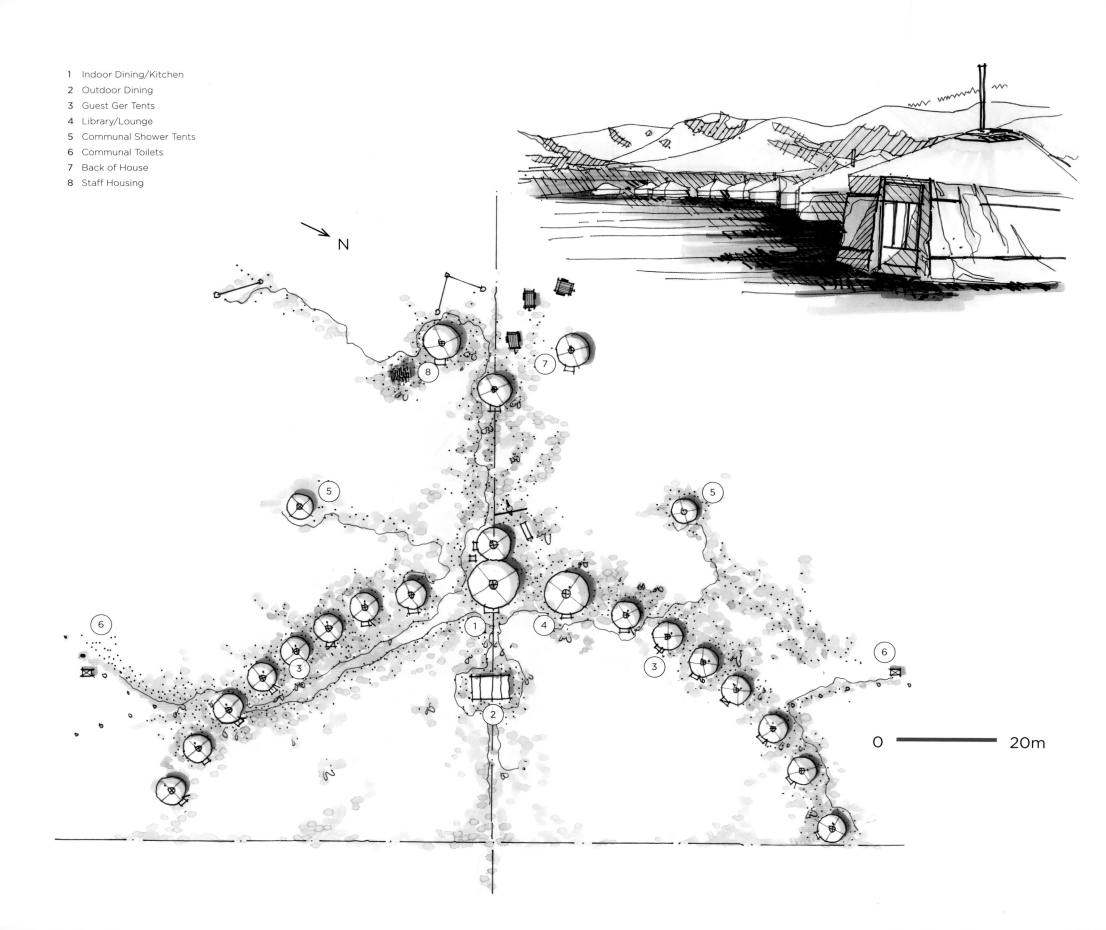

1 Indoor Dining/Kitchen
2 Outdoor Dining
3 Guest Ger Tents
4 Library/Lounge
5 Communal Shower Tents
6 Communal Toilets
7 Back of House
8 Staff Housing

N

0 ———————— 20m

down, packed up, and moved to another location, further proof that sometimes it really is all about the location. The camp is operational only from May through September to allow the existing ecosystems to regenerate.

ACTIVITIES: Activities include picnic day hikes to the lookout point of Hifte Gatsaa, yak cart riding, rafting, horseback riding, and mountain biking. The area is renowned as a haven for bird-watching, with avifauna ranging from the azure tits to the majestic steppe eagles. The camp also has an incredible, well-decorated library, with an exceptional collection of titles on Mongolia, China, and Russia.

A local native in traditional dress playing the horse-fiddle instrument with the white eco-camp in the background.

Opposite: Truly nomadic in form and function, the camp is seasonally broken down and set up. In true authentic fashion, yaks are used to move the camp. This page, clockwise from top left: Alive with color, the Upper Tuul River Valley is perfect for horseback riding, a favorite guest activity; The Spa-Tent located on the banks of the Tuul River; Colorful interior decorated in traditional colors, fabrics, and furnishings; Yaks are also used to transport water to the guest tents.

KNAPDALE ECOLODGE

NORTH ISLAND, NEW ZEALAND

DATE COMPLETED
2004

OWNERS
Kay and Kees Weytmans

ARCHITECT
Nicoll & Blackburne Architects

STRUCTURAL AND GEO-TECHNICAL ENGINEERS
JH Klimenko

ELECTRICAL ENGINEER
Jason Low Electrical

LANDSCAPE DESIGNERS
Natural Habitats and Escape Landscapes

Knapdale Ecolodge is located on the east coast of North Island, New Zealand, and near Gisborne, which is the first city in the world to greet the sun each day. At the two-bedroom Knapdale Ecolodge, guests get to experience a truly authentic rural lifestyle. The lodge is situated on a working farm, which is tended by a traditional Kiwi couple, Kay and Kees Weytmans. The experience is further enhanced by local Mâori guided visits to historic Whaitiripapa Pâ—the remains of an historic Mâori pâ (defensive earthworks)—located high in the hills of the 32 hectare (80 acre) Knapdale property. Members of the Gisborne-based Waka Toa Mâori cultural group welcome guests onto the two sacred sites and explain their history and significance; the group also entertains guests with an authentic performance on the eastern approach to Whaitiripapa Pâ with the Gisborne flats and the Pacific Ocean as a stunning background.

An exemplary model of the restoration of degraded native forests, Knapdale Ecolodge is the most intimate Mâori experience in New Zealand. Started sixteen years ago with closed canopy plantings of *Cupressus lusitanica*, *Pinus radiata*, and *Acacia melanoxylon*, Knapdale has become a sustainably managed, semi-permacultural operation with a variety of sustainable agro-forestry projects. At present about 10 hectares (25 acres) of the farm is a forest with a variety of native species. Unique to this endeavor is the fact the Knapdale is also a luxury ecolodge with a comprehensive selection of amenities and services.

Modern in design, Knapdale's environmentally friendly materials and technology leave as little an ecological footprint as possible—building timbers are non native and are sourced from a sustainable forest park; rainwater is harvested, stored in three large underground tanks, filtered, and used exclusively by the lodge; and hot water is provided by a large solar panel in summer and a wetback fire stove in winter. The passive solar under-floor heating system doesn't draw any electricity, and the mains power is produced at a nearby Tuai hydro

Previous spread: The lodge, in situ, amid an autumnal landscape. Opposite, top: A picture-perfect backdrop. Bottom: The ecolodge is just as beautiful in the summertime as during the fall. This page: View of the lodge with the organic garden visible in the distance.

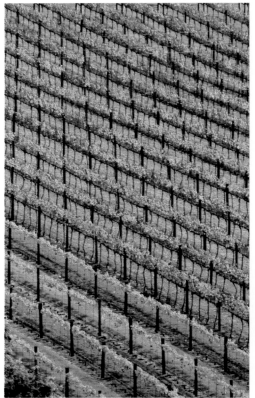

Above, top: Lodge garden and path to car park. Above: On-site vineyard. Right: The lounge opens to the outdoor terrace, the perfect environment for watching the sunset with a glass of local wine.

plant, which means the lodge is also entirely run on renewable resources. Additionally, gray waste water irrigates a small native tree plantation at the bottom of the garden, further proof that Knapdale is as environmentally sound as it is a unique experience.

CUISINE: Gourmet dinners are prepared according to guests' culinary preferences or dietary requirements. Guests can partake in the harvesting and production of the lodge's organically grown food, such as *camora*, a favorite local vegetable.

ACTIVITIES: Explore local wineries and sample some of the area's award-winning chardonnays. Visit the tiny beachside Mâori township of Whangara and marvel at the beautifully carved "Whale Rider" Whitireia meeting house. Surf one of the many east coast beaches or join professional forester Kees on a guided tour of pristine native forests and the internationally famous Eastwoodhill Arboretum.

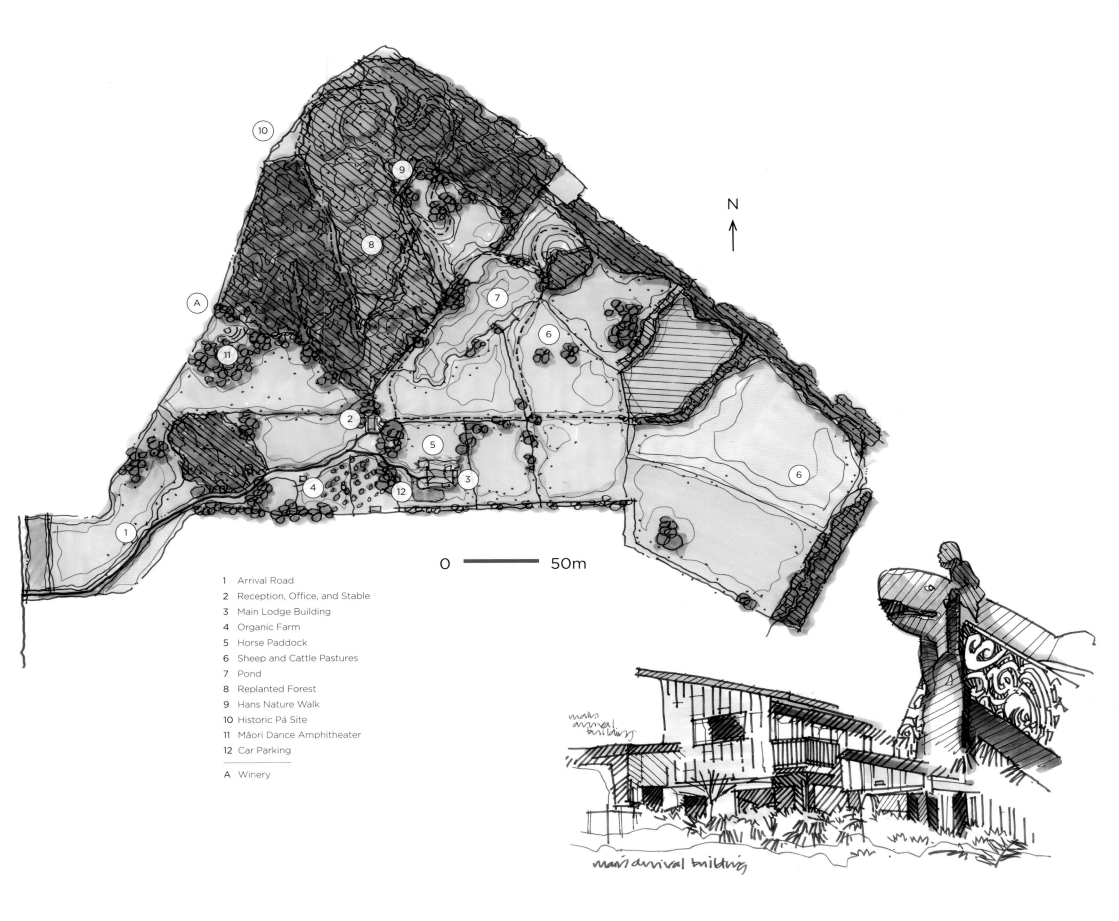

N

1 Arrival Road
2 Reception, Office, and Stable
3 Main Lodge Building
4 Organic Farm
5 Horse Paddock
6 Sheep and Cattle Pastures
7 Pond
8 Replanted Forest
9 Hans Nature Walk
10 Historic Pá Site
11 Mâori Dance Amphitheater
12 Car Parking

A Winery

0 ———— 50m

main arrival building

CRISTALINO JUNGLE LODGE

MATO GROSSO, BRAZIL

DATE COMPLETED
1992

OWNER
Vitoria da Riva Carvalho (Brazil)

ARCHITECT (BUNGALOWS)
Adriana Da Riva (Brazil)

STRUCTURAL ENGINEER (OBSERVATION TOWER)
George S. Suli (Brazil)

PERMACULTURIST
Addie Da Riva Carvalho (Brazil)

1 Arrival Boat Dock
2 Main Lodge Building
3 Guide Rooms/Library
4 Guest Bungalows
5 Sun Deck
6 Forest Trail
7 Kitchen/Staff Dining
8 Organic Garden
9 Back of House
10 Staff Housing

A Cristalino River

N

0 ⎯⎯⎯ 30m

The Cristalino Jungle Lodge is located on the southern edge of the Brazilian Amazon rain forest, between the upper reaches of the Tapajós and Xingu rivers. This area of land is known not only for its rich biodiversity, but also for its varied jungle topography of pristine forest and dense, aquatic habitat, making it an Amazonian sanctuary unlike any in the world. Already internationally famous as a destination spot for bird and butterfly enthusiasts—the lodge has more than 550 bird species and at least 2,000 butterfly species on more than 7,720 hectares (19,075 acres) of preserved, private land—the Cristalino Jungle Lodge is making a name for itself as a place for ecoadventurers, boasting an extensive trail system and a clean, black-water river, perfect for canoeing and swimming.

Accessible only by boat, the lodge itself is flanked on all sides with tropical forest, making it feel like a true jungle sanctuary and giving guests a unique opportunity to experience full immersion in this wild ecosystem. Meant to harmonize with the surrounding forest and built with respect for the surrounding ecosystems, the lodge's ecofriendly bungalows adhere to sustainable practices: All the buildings were sited in already disturbed areas, foundations were dug by hand, no heavy machinery was used during construction. In addition, solar power provides energy for certain needs; cleaning products are biodegradable; guests are encouraged to reuse towels; permaculture biological waste-water treatments exist for both black- and gray-water disposal; and organic and nonorganic disposal systems compost and

recycle most materials. In an effort to maintain sustainable trail management, activities are limited to eight people per trail, minimizing any negative impact on the land and guaranteeing personalized attention and a unique experience for all. Dedicated to improving the lives of the local community as much as servicing the needs of guests, the lodge supports the Cristalino Ecological Foundation, a nonprofit organization that works with educational and conservation issues in the region. One such project is the School of the Amazon, which promotes environmental education workshops for local children. With its comprehensive education, preservation, and conservation programs, and exotic tropical locale, the Cristalino Jungle Lodge combines the wild of the jungle with the sustainability of living green.

CUISINE: Traditional Brazilian cuisine is prepared in a wood stove, and delicacies are wrapped in banana leaves and roasted over an open fire. All dinners are candle-lit and organic fruits and vegetables are offered when available.

ACTIVITIES: More than 20 kilometers (12 miles) of well-maintained trails that pass through a variety of habitats give guests the opportunity to experience the local Amazonian flora and fauna firsthand. The Cristalino area supports rich wildlife, including tapirs, peccaries, deer, capybaras, and primates. For ecoadventurers, main activities include rock-climbing, canoe expeditions, and forest camping.

Previous spread: The lodge's outdoor sun deck, stretching into the Cristalino River. This page, clockwise from top left: Guest reading a novel on the sun-deck; A romantic candle-lit dinner in the thatched dining cabana; Outdoor showers in the guest bungalows.

ON THE DRAWING BOARDS

The ecolodges in the following pages represents future ecolodge projects from all around the world, all of which are in different stages of development. Some are still under construction, while others are in planning and design stages. In rare instances, prototypes only exist. All of these ecolodges, however, share a commonality: In their own individual way, they each point toward the future of ecolodges and ecotourism. They are the up-and-comers, the new kids on the block who are shaping and helping to define the new generation of authentic ecolodges.

The question is not what you look at, but what you see.
—Henry David Thoreau

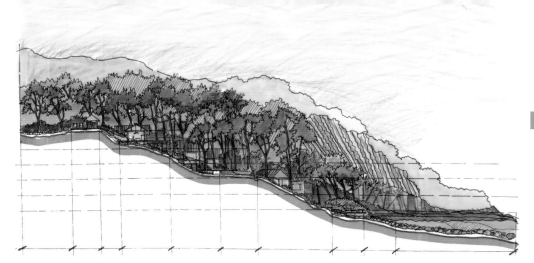

KWANARI ECOLODGE

RICHMOND BAY, COMMONWEALTH OF DOMINICA

OWNER Kasswebb Ltd. CONSULTANT TEAM LEADER Hitesh Mehta (Kenya/ United States) DESIGN ARCHITECT AND LANDSCAPE ARCHITECT HM Design (United States) ARCHITECT OF RECORD Joffre Greene (Dominica) STRUCTURAL AND CIVIL ENGINEERS CEP Partnership (Dominica) ELECTRICAL AND MECHANICAL ENGINEERS Genivar (Trinidad) INTERIOR DESIGN Kelly LaPlante Organic Interior Design Inc (United States) QUANTITY SURVEYOR Derek Angol (Dominica) PROJECT MANAGER Lenny Andre (Dominica) ECOPSYCHOLOGIST Terri Henry (Dominica)

Kwanari Ecolodge is located on the eastern side of Dominica and 10 kilometers (6 miles) south of the only Native American territory in the Caribbean—Kalinago. The project site occupies approximately 2.8 hectares (7 acres), and is the first master planned and designed ecolodge in Dominica with an international consultant team that represents several continents. The total development includes a wellness center, forest and ocean villas, tree house, infinity swimming pool, library, conference hall, and trails.

HM Design is introducing a whole new style of architecture to the Caribbean— Forest Caribbean—which is a hybrid of the classic Caribbean architecture (with its intricate fretwork, balconies, dormer windows) and the "cabin in the woods" (logs, stone, rustic, contextual design) architecture prevalent in North America and Europe. Every aspect of the lodge revolves around the site's most striking quality: the meeting of forest and sea. Every building has a theme that connects it with either the secondary forest or the Atlantic Ocean. The lodge treads lightly, respecting the site's topography, hydrology, flora, and fauna, and allowing all natural systems to function and grow uninterrupted. The project will be a showcase for the crafts of the local communities and the Kalinago peoples themselves are constructing the indigenous-inspired *mouinas* (gazebos).

Kwanari Ecolodge is under construction and scheduled to open in August 2011.

CANALETE RANCH

CATAGENA DE INDIAS, COLOMBIA

OWNER Colinas San Simeon S.A.   SUSTAINABLE MASTER PLANNER HM Design (United States)   ARCHITECT Simon Velez (Colombia)

Canalete Ranch is currently a 1,040 hectare (2,569 acre) working cattle farm located 10 kilometers (6 miles) north of the town of Cartagena de Indias on the Caribbean coast of Colombia. Surrounding Canalete EcoRanch are several Afro-Caribbean villages, such as Tierra Lugo and Bayunca. Apart from the cattle grazing, holding, and feeding areas, there are several ponds, streams, fragmented woodlands, and, most importantly, the only stand of pristine rain forest 300 hectares (720 acres) within a 500 kilometer (312 mile) radius of Cartagena. The forward-thinking developers' vision is to create an authentic ecologically and socially friendly "conservation community" at Canalete EcoRanch.

The developers have jump-started the development with several flagship projects designed by the world's topmost bamboo architect, Simon Velez: a nondenominational water temple, a horse stable, a cattle-viewing corral, a horsekeeper's house, a horse-viewing pavilion, and two four-bedroom homes, one of which is for a member of the development team. Currently, an overall sustainable community-focused master plan is being prepared that would add to the existing amenities. The total build out includes a luxury ecolodge, private ecovillas, recreational components, wellness center, school, health clinic, and links golf course using innovative technology for the preservation of the environment. A phasing plan will take into consideration the need for integrated development of tourist accommodation, activities, services, transportation, and other infrastructural development within the site.

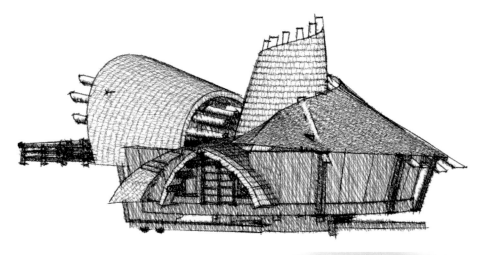

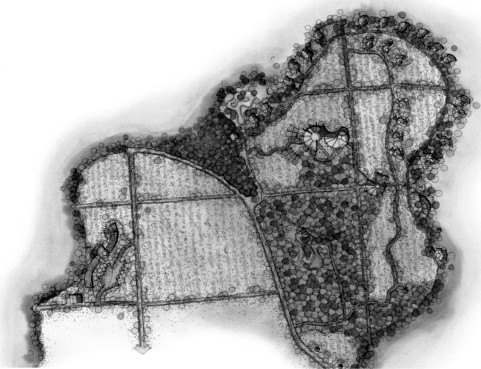

NYUNGWE FOREST ECOLODGE

NYUNGWE FOREST NATIONAL PARK, RWANDA

OWNER **ORTPN** CONSULTANT TEAM LEADER **Hitesh Mehta (Kenya/United States)** MASTER PLANNER, CONCEPT ARCHITECT, AND LANDSCAPE ARCHITECT **HM Design (United States)** ARCHITECT OF RECORD **Studio Infinity (Kenya)** STRUCTURAL AND CIVIL ENGINEERS **Hardip Singh Sura (Kenya)** ELECTRICAL ENGINEER **Elemech Consultants (Kenya)** MECHANICAL ENGINEER **Hydro Solutions (Kenya)** INTERIOR DESIGN **Decor (Kenya)** QUANTITY SURVEYOR **Tandem and Stark (Kenya)** PROJECT MANAGER **Lakes Consortium (Kenya)**

Nyungwe Forest Ecolodge is proposed to be located in a tea plantation at the edge of 870 square kilometer (335 square mile) Nyungwe Forest National Park, Southwest Rwanda. Nyungwe Forest is the largest Afro-Montane forest in Africa, is one of only two places in the world that harbor twelve species of primates, and is one of the most ancient forests, dating back to before the last ice age. A uniquely rich center of floral diversity, the forest has more than two hundred different types of trees, and a myriad of flowering plants, including the otherworldly giant lobelia and a host of colorful orchids.

A full-fledged international consultant team planned, designed, and supervised the first stages of construction until the twenty-five-unit lodge was bought by Dubai World, who used a different set of consultants to create a typical nature lodge. It should be noted that the current lodge bears no resemblance to this case study. The master plan proposed four different types of luxury villas, tree houses, wellness center, conference center, nature activity center, library, and trails.

The principles of form, landscaping, and color have been given particular attention in addressing such issues of physical and cultural context. Local Rwandese architectural building typology has inspired the forms of Nyungwe Forest Ecolodge and the main concepts have all been derived from either patterns present in the forest or cultural artifacts; the floor plans of the main villas resemble the spiral energy embodied in a young forest fern, for example. Materials proposed—volcanic stone, brick, wood shingles, eucalyptus poles, local mats, and pots—are all locally sourced.

The construction of Nyungwe Ecolodge is on hold due to financial and market forces.

ARIO ECORANCH

NICOYA PENINSULA, COSTA RICA

OWNER Grupo Bongo Ario SA   CONSULTANT TEAM LEADER Hitesh Mehta (Kenya/United States)   SUSTAINABLE MASTER PLANNERS HM Design (United States) and 40 North (Costa Rica)   COMMUNITY SPECIALIST Ana Baez (Costa Rica)   ECOLOGIST Viviana Ruiz-Gutierrez (Costa Rica)   ECOPSYCHOLOGIST Terri Henry (Dominica)

The 2,000 hectare (4,940 acre) property is situated along a large fertile river valley comprised of the Bongo and Ario rivers and forms part of the largest watershed in the Nicoya Peninsula. Ario Ecoranch will be a sustainable resort community development backed by the vision of its sole owner, the Grew family. Ario Ecoranch seeks to become a global model in eco-community development that integrates social, economic, ecological, and spiritual considerations for the long-term benefit of local ecosystems and peoples.

The consultant team worked closely with the client family to prepare a sustainable master tourism plan for the whole property. The several-phased development plan includes a high-end twenty-five-villa ecolodge and wellness center, rental pool homes, pool, stables, polo field, family estate, research station, ranger post, library, and trails. To support this master plan vision, the family has created CIRENAS, a U.S. nonprofit organization, which actively links outside visitors and students with local residents in service-learning projects, estuary and forest habitat conservation efforts, a botanical sanctuary, and a newly built ranger station.

The schematic phase of the first-phase development has already been completed.

RIGON ECOLODGE

SOUTH LOANGO NATIONAL PARK, GABON

CLIENT Conservation International (CI)   SUSTAINABLE MASTER PLANNER EDSA (United States)   ARCHITECT Hitesh Mehta (Kenya/United States)
ECOTOURISM SPECIALISTS Costas Christ (United States) and Kaddu Sebunya (Uganda)   MARKETING ANALYST Roger Lefrancois (Canada)
WILDLIFE BEHAVIORIST Craig Sholley (United States)   COMMUNITY TOURISM SPECIALIST Pamela Wight (Canada)

Rigon Ecolodge is planned to be located just north of the village of Sette Cama and at the edge of Loango National Park, the crown jewel in the Gabon National Park system. It is proposed to be a world-class, upscale, low-impact accommodation facility that is not only environmentally and socially friendly, but also provides a quality interpretive experience. The recommendations by the architect were for the existing dilapidated lodge to be demolished and materials and equipment to be salvaged and reused in the new lodge. The new buildings will be in visual harmony with their natural surroundings and will not intrude upon the physical landscape as foreign structures.

Rigon Ecolodge will consist of ten luxuriously designed and decorated villas, reception/lounge/dining area, nature activity center, a small swimming pool, library, canopy walk, and meditation gazebos by the lagoon. The 150 meter (500 foot) long canopy walk will be the first one of its kind in Central Africa and will be located just inside the park. Viewers will be able to observe three very distinct vegetation types and the corresponding species that inhabit them—including those species that spend all their time above the canopy.

The lodge implementation is currently in need of a private sector partnership.

SABYINYO ECOLODGE
KINIGI, RWANDA

CLIENT International Gorilla Conservation Partnership (IGCP)   SUSTAINABLE MASTER PLANNER EDSA (United States)   ARCHITECT Hitesh Mehta (Kenya/United States)
COMMUNITY TOURISM SPECIALIST Christine Guchu-Katee (Kenya)

Sabyinyo Ecolodge site is located several kilometers west of Kinigi town and close to the edge of Parc National des Volcans (PNV). The site location is one of the most beautiful in this region. From the top of the site, all of the six Virunga volcanoes are visible on a clear day. Sabyinyo Ecolodge is to be used as a base from which guests will drive to the Virunga National Park boundary and begin their treks to observe mountain gorillas and rare golden monkeys. Guests at the ecolodge will also have the added benefit of staying overnight at a satellite-tented camp planned to be located at the northern shores of Lake Burera. One of the main purposes of developing the ecolodge and tented camp is to demonstrate how tourism can help elevate the livelihood of local people. The ownership of the lodge and tented camp will rest with the respective local communities, while the management and marketing will be undertaken by a

private sector partner. Funds from the tourism projects would go through the local districts for community development.

The site plan is experiential and takes into consideration the varying views: from the car park to the reception and then to either the luxury villa or to the dining/lounge areas. Designed to be built entirely with local materials and by local craftsmen using alternative forms of energy, water conservation, and sewage treatment, Sabyinyo Ecolodge was designed to become the flagship eco-accommodation facility in Central Africa. Eucalyptus poles are used to great effect to create roof lines that mimic the slope angles of the Sabyinyo Volcano, at the base of which the ecolodge was proposed to be located.

There is currently a lodge on this site but it has no resemblance to the planning and design approach above.

SHALTA ECOLODGE

AL GHAT NATIONAL PARK, SAUDI ARABIA

CLIENT Supreme Council of Tourism (SCT) SUSTAINABLE MASTER PLANNER EDSA and Planning Charette Participants (United States) ARCHITECT Hitesh Mehta and Design Charette Participants (Kenya/United States) CULTURAL AND ARCHITECTURAL HERITAGE EXPERT Dr. Ali Al-Anbar (Saudi Arabia) TOURISM PRODUCT SPECIALIST Keith Sproule (United States)

EDSA, a landscape architecture and planning firm based in Florida was the facilitator and team leader for the preparation of conceptual plans for Shalta Ecolodge, Al Ghat National Park, located three hours north of the capital, Riyadh. Following a site visit, all the drawings that were produced were the result of a four-day participatory ecolodge workshop comprised of local community, professionals, and members of the Supreme Commission of Tourism. The program for the ecolodge, which is sited overlooking a seasonal waterfall and facing the rising sun, includes private accommodation areas, presidential suite, environmental utility learning area, nature center, and public spaces, such as reception, lounge, and dining areas.

The Shalta site has all the regional ingredients for a successful ecolodge: There are unique old Nejdi villages (Al Ghat and Al Majma'ah) with rich architectural heritages, the national park is a protected area, and the opportunities for interpretations are numerous. The whole ecolodge will celebrate local Nejdi vernacular architecture to reflect its context with the desert surroundings and only locally available materials will be used to build the ecolodge. The proposal is to establish a development "credo" for the ecolodge that will give it a distinct identity among ecolodges in Saudi Arabia. The utmost intention is to encourage respectful development that takes into consideration both environmental and social Islamic concerns such as defined areas for men, women, and children.

Shalta Ecolodge was a "model" ecolodge exercise and hopefully will advance to the next stage of development.

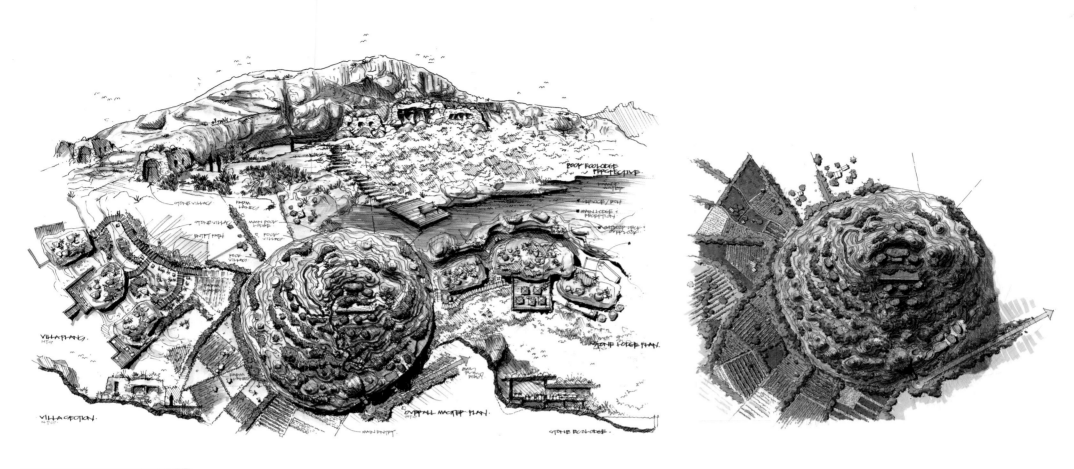

MWIBALE ROCK LODGE

BUNGOMA DISTRICT, KENYA

OWNER **Local Community**   SUSTAINABLE MASTER PLANNER **EDSA (United States)**   ARCHITECT **Hitesh Mehta (Kenya/United States)**
COMMUNITY ECOTOURISM SPECIALIST **John Ochola (Kenya)**

Mwibale Rock Lodge is located to the south of Bungoma town on a rock promontory (Mwibale Rock Hill) within Bungoma District, Western Kenya. The lodge will have a capacity of twenty beds and a cultural center that will be used by all the Luhya subtribes for cultural entertainment. Other amenities include an outdoor amphitheater and a gazebo to be located at the top of the rock hill.

Only environmentally friendly materials sourced from the region will be used on the project: Rock from the existing site will completely camouflage the lodge within the hill, and all external materials will be natural—wood, stone, or grass—their earth colors making the lodge blend further into its surroundings. Water will be captured from the existing dam, filtered, and used for drinking, washing, and cooking, and dry composting toilets will be used to save water. Energy will be conserved through use of solar power and candles. Unskilled and semiskilled construction workers will be sourced from the immediate community while skilled staff will be sourced nationally. Handicrafts, pottery, and other cultural products will be purchased from the whole of Western Province.

Mwibale Rock Lodge will be developed using a partnership model: Donors will provide initial seed funding, the private sector will build and operate the lodge, and the local community will provide the land, labor, and materials.

The lodge implementation is currently in need of a private sector partnership.

DIRECTORY OF ECOLODGES

ADRÈRE AMELLAL
Web site: www.adrereamellal.net

BASECAMP MAASAI MARA
Web site: www.basecampexplorer.com/
our_destinations/masai_mara/our_
basecamps/125177?expand=6

BAY OF FIRES LODGE
Web site: www.bayoffireslodge.com.au

CAMPI YA KANZI
Web site: www.kapawi.com

CANOPY TOWERS
Web site: www.canopytower.com

COCONUT LAGOON
Web site: www.cghearth.com/coconut_
lagoon/index.htm

CHALALAN ECOLODGE
Web Site: www.chalalan.com

CHUMBE ISLAND ECOLODGE
Web site: www.chumbeisland.com

CONCORDIA ECO-TENTS
Web site: www.maho.org/concordia.cfm

CREE VILLAGE ECOLODGE
Web site: www.creevillage.com

CRISTALINO JUNGLE LODGE
Web site: www.cristalinolodge.com.br

CROSSWATERS ECOLODGE
Web site: www.crosswaters.net.cn

DAINTREE ECOLODGE AND SPA
Web site: www.daintree-ecolodge.com.au

DAMARALAND CAMP
Web site: www.wilderness-safaris.com/
namibia_kunene/damaraland_camp/
introduction/

ECOLODGE RENDEZ-VOUS
Web site: www.ecolodge-saba.com

FEYNAN ECOLODGE
Web site: www.rscn.org.
jo/orgsite/wj/Group2/
CampsiteslodgesandGuesthouses/
tabid/171/default.aspx#611

GULUDO BEACH LODGE
Web site: www.guludo.com

IL NGWESI LODGE
Web site: www.ilngwesi.com

JALMAN MEADOWS GER CAMP
Web site: www.nomadicjourneys.com/
index.php?option=com_content&task=vi
ew&id=55&Itemid=99

KAPAWI ECOLODGE
Web site: www.kapawi.com

KASBAH DU TOUBKAL
Web site: www.kasbahdutoubkal.com

KAYA MAWA
Web Site: www.kayamawa.com

KNAPDALE ECOLODGE
Website: www.knapdale.co.nz

LAPA RIOS ECOLODGE
Web site: www.laparios.com

LAS TORRES ECOCAMP
Web site: www.cascada.travel/places/
programs.php?IDP=142&ID=100&OP=1

THE LODGE AT CHAA CREEK
Web site: www.chaacreek.com

MOSETLHA BUSH CAMP
Web site: www.thebushcamp.com

NIHIWATU
Web site: www.nihiwatu.com

PHINDA FOREST LODGE
Web site: www.andbeyondafrica.
com/luxury_safari/south_africa/
phinda_private_game_reserve/and_
beyond_phinda_private_game_reserve/
accommodation/and_beyond_phinda_
forest_lodge

RANWELI HOLIDAY VILLAGE
Web site: www.ranweli.com

SHOMPOLE
Web site: www.shompole.com

SIX SENSES HIDEAWAY NINH VAN BAY
Web site: www.sixsenses.com/Six-
Senses-Hideaway-Ninh-Van-Bay/
index.php

SUKAU RAINFOREST LODGE
Web site: www.sukau.com

TOURINDIA KETTUVALLAM
HOUSEBOATS
Web Site: www.tourindiaonline.com

URUYÉN LODGE
Web site: www.angelconservation.org/
lodges.html

WILDERNESS LODGE ARTHUR'S PASS
Web site: www.wildernesslodge.co.nz/
wildernesslodge/arthurs-pass/

ABOUT THE AUTHOR

Hitesh Mehta is one of the world's leading authorities, practitioners, and researchers on ecotourism physical planning and both the landscape architectural and architectural aspects of ecolodges. Hitesh is President of Florida-based HM Design and has provided environmental planning, landscape architectural, and architectural consultancy in over fifty countries around the world. *National Geographic Adventure* magazine has identified Hitesh as one of five Sustainable Tourism Pioneers in the world and he was named by *Men's Journal* as one of the "Twenty-five Most Powerful People in Adventure" in the world. He is the longest serving board member of The International Ecotourism Society and is one of the founding members of The Ecotourism Society of Kenya. Mr. Mehta is also a professional photographer and a Cricket Hall of Fame player in Kenya, Africa.

ABOUT THE CONTRIBUTORS

Matthew Lewis is a professional illustrator. As Design Director at Landscape Architecture and Planning firm 40NORTH, Matthew Lewis has extensive experience in the planning and design of resort projects around the world with an emphasis on sustainable planning and ecotourism. Prior to joining 40NORTH in January 2008, he was a Senior Associate with EDSA for a variety of resort projects in Asia, the Middle East, the Caribbean, and Africa. In addition to his experience in the Fort Lauderdale, Florida, office, he spent a year and a half living and working in Beijing, China.

Costas Christ is internationally recognized as one of the pioneers of ecotourism, whose work has taken him to more than one hundred countries across six continents. He is the Editor-at-Large for *National Geographic Traveler* and serves as Chairman of the World Travel and Tourism Council-Tourism for Tomorrow Awards, which recognize global leadership in sustainable tourism. He is a frequent keynote speaker at international travel conferences and he has appeared on the *Today* show, *Good Morning America*, the Travel Channel, and National Public Radio to talk about a new vision for the tourism industry.

ACKNOWLEDGMENTS

This book would not have been possible without the support and help of many individuals. So to these people I say a big thank you. In particular, I want to thank my former employer, EDSA (Landscape Architecture and Planning Company), whose board gave me full support over a period of ten years and in so doing contributed hugely to the development and advancement of the field of ecotourism and ecolodge planning. EDSA's efforts have been immense and should not go unnoticed. Others who supported and helped me along the way include the following:

Signe Bergstrom
Lisa Sharkey
Matt Lewis
Chang Du
Minoo Rahbar
Ravi Ruparel
Penny Urquhart
Faye Kass
Terri Henry
Heather Arrowood
Yolanda Barquil
Katie Boyle
Sejal Shah
Sachin Shah
Melanie Bell
Sharon Swift
Lodge owners, operators, and guides

My apologies if I have missed anyone else.